Understanding Yourself and Ot

UNDERSTANDING YOURSELF AND OTHERS®

An Introduction
TO INTERACTION STYLES

LINDA V. BERENS

Telos
PUBLICATIONS
Huntington Beach
CALIFORNIA

Copyright ©2001 Linda V. Berens

All rights reserved. No portion of this publication may be reproduced, distributed, stored in a retrieval system, or transmitted in any form or by any means, including electronic, mechanical, photocopying, recording, or otherwise, without the prior written permission of the publisher, except in the case of brief quotations embodied in critical reviews and certain other noncommercial uses permitted by copyright law. For permission requests, write to the publisher, addressed "Attention: Permission Coordinator," at the address below.

PRINTED IN CANADA

Understanding Yourself and Others is a registered trademark of Telos Publications, Huntington Beach, California.

The Self-Discovery Process and *The TRI Methodology* are registered trademarks of Temperament Research Institute, Huntington Beach, California.

Myers-Briggs Type Indicator and *MBTI* are registered trademarks of Consulting Psychologists Press, Inc., Palo Alto, California.

DiSC is a registered trademark of Inscape Publishing, Inc., Minneapolis, MN.

Published By:
Telos Publications
P.O. Box 4457, Huntington Beach, California 92605-4457
714.668.1818 or 866.416.8973 / fax 714.668.1100
http://www.telospublications.com
International Standard Book Number: 0–9712144-0-9

05 04 03 02 01   10 9 8 7 6 5 4 3 2 1

Cover Photo: Red Maple Leaves on the Robert Frost Trail, Vermont ©Tim Fitzharris/Minden Pictures, used with permission.
Cover/Layout Design/Illustrations: Visibility Designs, Fountain Valley, California – http://www.visibilitydesigns.com
Illustrations: Chris Berens of Thumbnail Productions

Ordering Information

Individual Sales U.S.: This publication can be purchased directly from the Telos Publications Web site or at the address above.

Individual Sales International: A list of international distributors can be received directly from the Telos Publications Web site or at the address above.

Quantity Sales: Special discounts are available on quantity purchases by corporations, associations, and others. Details can be received at the Telos Publications Web site or at the address above.

Orders for College Textbook/Course Adoption Use: Information can be received directly from the Telos Publications Web site or at the address above.

Orders by U.S./International Trade Bookstores and Wholesalers: Information can be received directly from the Telos Publications Web site or at the address above.

Training is available for further exploration of the information provided in this book.
   Contact:
   Temperament Research Institute (TRI)
   http://www.tri-network.com
   1-800-700-4TRI or 1-714-841-0041

TRI provides a certification curriculum for *The TRI Methodology*® and *The Self-Discovery Process*®, organizational consulting and in-house training for communication, team building, leadership development, coaching, and organizational development, and is an approved provider of the *Myers-Briggs Type Indicator*® (*MBTI*®) Qualification Programs and MBTI Certification Continuing Education Programs.

This book is dedicated to
- My colleagues and my students who have found value in the seeds of this work and who encouraged me to pursue it.
- David Keirsey who planted the seeds and gave me a framework for understanding personality from an organismic view and an interactional view.
- John Berens for putting aside his own needs to provide a safe haven for creativity—a truly fertile soil.
- Kris Kiler who nurtured the seeds and tilled the soil so they could grow.

Acknowledgments

A theory doesn't develop in a vacuum. Originality always comes through interaction with the ideas of others, in books and in person. Many thanks to
- Kris Kiler for pushing me to make the links to the other models and actually get something on paper!
- Dario Nardi, for dialoging with me in theoryland to broaden my understandings and for helping me compose and edit the descriptions. Your ability to cut to the essential while noticing what's missing are forever valued.
- Linda Ernst and Melissa Smith for helping teach this model in our workshops and for sharing your stories from your own clients. Your contributions are too many to even begin to detail.
- Scott Campbell for pushing me to get at the fundamentals of the pattern, helping me do so, and continuing to test drive the work with your clients.
- Stephanie Kiler, Connie Coppoth, Kris Kiler, and Lynne Berens for putting up with working in a learning laboratory and being willing to examine our conflicts in light of this model.
- All of the TRI affiliates who read descriptions and had friends and colleagues read descriptions. I fear if I name you, I'll leave someone out.
- The many people over the years who said, "This could be a theory on its own." Your vision and encouragement is now realized.

About the Author

Linda V. Berens

Linda V. Berens, Ph.D., is the director and founder of Temperament Research Institute (TRI), which provides organizational consulting and interventions as well as certification of trainers in The TRI Methodology™. TRI is one of seven organizations that provide Qualification Programs for the Myers-Briggs Type Indicator®, the most widely used personality instrument in the world. Linda is the author of *Understanding Yourself and Others®: An Introduction to Temperament* and *Dynamics of Personality Type: Understanding and Applying Jung's Cognitive Processes* and the coauthor of *The 16 Personality Types: Descriptions for Self-Discovery* and *Working Together: A Personality-Centered Approach to Management*. She is an organizational consultant and has spent over twenty-five years teaching professionals as well as helping individuals and teams recognize their strengths, transcend their weaknesses, and work together better. Linda is recognized internationally for her theoretical contributions to the field of psychological type and for developing user-friendly training materials for practical application of understanding individual differences.

Contents

A Word from the Author iv

Introduction 1
   Why 1

Coming to Know Your "Self" 2
   History of the Four Interaction Style Patterns 2
   Personality Instruments 2
   Self-Discovery 3

The Nature of Interaction Styles 4
   Interaction Style Is Inborn 4
   Interaction Style Remains Constant 4
   Interaction Style Drives Behavior 5
   Interaction Style Is Dynamic, Not Static Influencing, Not Limiting 5
   Interaction Style Is a Pattern 6
   Interaction Style Is Organic 6
   Interaction Style Is a Communication 6

Exploring Your Interaction Style 7
   Using Your Experiences 7
   Four Interaction Styles 8
   What Fits? 9

Behind-the-Scenes Interaction Style 10
Chart-the-Course Interaction Style 12
Get-Things-Going Interaction Style 14
In-Charge Interaction Style 16
Clarifying Your Interaction Style 18
   Things-in-Common 18
   Communication—Ways We Influence Others 19
   Roles—Ways to Define Relationships 21
   Attention—Focus and Interest 22

Patterns of Interaction Styles 23
   The Four Interaction Style Patterns 23

The Interaction Style Arrows 24
   The Graphic Representation 24

Identifying Others 26
Perspective Shifting 28
   Energy Shifting Tips 28
   Aspects of an Interaction 28
   Interaction Styles and Stress 30

Where Do You Go from Here? 31
   Honor the Differences in Yourself 31
   Honor the Differences in Others 31
   Welcome the Diversity 31

Appendix A: Essential Qualities of the Patterns 32
Appendix B: Frequently Asked Questions 36
Appendix C: Links to Other Models 37
Appendix D: References 39

A Word from the Author

History

Our development of the Interaction Style Model was sparked by a presentation in 1985 by Dr. David Keirsey, a gestalt-field systems psychologist and developer of Keirseyan Temperament Theory. As he studied the four basic temperament patterns that have been observed for over twenty-five centuries, he noticed that they seem to take two different kinds of roles in their interactions with each other. Thus there are two varieties of each temperament, role directive and role informative. He later expanded the variations to two more, based on a distinction of whether people tend to initiate in establishing new relationships or respond to the initiations of others.

For several years, we used these distinctions as very brief explanations that helped us bridge from the four Keirseyan Temperaments (Artisan, Guardian, Rational, and Idealist) to the sixteen types designated by the four-letter type code. We found they helped people find a better fit among the sixteen type patterns and we also saw some relationships with the then-new literature on differences in communication patterns between men and women. We also noticed some very strong similarities between the dimensions of the DiSC® Personal Profile System and the Social Styles literature based in the work of Dr. David Merrill. When I reviewed the behavioral styles literature, I found these styles mapped well to the four social styles, although each of the descriptions was heavily weighted toward at least one of the Keirseyan temperament patterns.

As we worked to understand and explain these distinctions, we observed four distinct interaction styles. Steeped in holistic observation methods, organismic psychology, gestalt-field-systems psychology, family systems, and organizational systems, I knew these must be patterns rather than mere dichotomous dimensions. Kris Kiler urged me to develop the descriptions themselves. Then Dr. Dario Nardi pointed out that we were indeed using a multiple-models method (as practiced in systems science) to help people find their best-fit type pattern. Well, if it was a model, then I decided I'd better research its foundations. A more detailed explanation of the foundations and links can be found in Appendix C.

Our Method

As Robert and Dorothy Bolton point out

> An elegant model is a useful simplification of reality. It enables you to ignore a mass of irrelevant or less relevant details so you can focus on what is most important. A model shows what to look for, helps identify meaningful patterns, and aids in interpreting what you see
>
> —p. 9 People Styles at Work*

I was exposed to the DiSC® instrument in the early 1980s and did not find a fit for myself in it. I dismissed it as fuzzy categories. I tried to read the book that was the root of the model, *Emotions of Normal People* by William Marston, but couldn't see the connections. It seemed that all of the trait model descriptions like DiSC, as well as the social styles or behavioral styles, included a mix of the Keirseyan Temperament Theory information. Some styles, like "D" or "Driver" were predominantly Rational (ENTJ variety) or Artisan (ESTP variety) and "C" or "Analytical" were predominantly Guardian (ISTJ variety) or Rational (INTJ variety).

I used temperament and the sixteen type patterns to filter out the characteristics that were particular to certain types as I read and integrated the descriptions. I found Bolton and Bolton's descriptions the most helpful, but found nuggets in the other sources as well (see Resources section, page 39). The test was that if my hypothesis was right, a pattern that fit ENTJ, ESTJ, ESTP, and ENFJ types would emerge that had no reference to any of the four temperaments of these types, and so on for the other three Interaction Style patterns. Indeed it did.

Testing of the Descriptions

The descriptions were tested against best-fit type, not merely a result from the MBTI® instrument. As I drafted the descriptions, I made sure people of each type were not put off by the description for their Interaction Style pattern and they would choose it as fitting better than any of the other three descriptions. These descriptions have been circulated and tested in workshops and with family and friends for over a year. Each piece of feedback has been run against a filter of "Is this something that comes from their temperament pattern and their full type pattern or would each of the four types who share the interaction style agree?" Then the descriptions were edited and tested again.

We Need Your Help

Now it is time to publish the descriptions and the characteristics of the Interaction Style Model. And I do so with some trepidation. I know there will be some users of psychological type who will not be able to let go of some of their closely held definitions and models to see this model for what it is. And, I am also not completely an expert in the social styles, DiSC models, or traditional biologically based temperament research. Yet, we have found this knowledge so helpful in the day-to-day operations of our living laboratory at TRI and our graduates are so eager to have the resource that we can delay no longer. Please know this is a dynamic, growing work and there will be a version 2.0 with the help of your feedback. Please let us know how the ideas, frameworks, descriptions, and practical suggestions in this book work for you.

---

*People Styles at Work, Robert Bolton and Dorothy Grover Bolton. (Palo Alto, Calif.: National Press Books, 1963), 10–12.

Introduction

Why?

BLM, BLT, Stress, and Other Ills

It seems most of the stress and conflict in our lives is related to how we interact with others. We all seem to have one of two disorders, BLM Syndrome or BLT Syndrome. Some of us have both of these disorders and they alternate. Others have just one operating most of the time. They are not really curable, but we can learn about them, control for them, and reduce their symptoms.

BLM stands for Be Like Me. We all expect others to be like us and are really surprised when they are not. Then, of course, we say they are wrong, bad, or even weird and crazy. BLM leads us heavily into the "blame game," where anyone who is not like us is to blame for what goes wrong.

BLT stands for Be Like Them. Often we get into a position of feeling like we are not good enough the way we are and we must be like someone else. Advertising feeds us images of how we should be, as do cultural and gender stereotypes. BLT gets us into the "self-blame game."

The Way Out?

So what is the way out of these never ending games that lead to unproductive behavior and unhappy people? An understanding of yourself and others! How are you different from others? How are you the same? Why do you seem driven to do things a certain way, even when that way is not working?

Understanding your natural Interaction Style will help you see how you are okay just the way you are and how to use your personal strengths for maximum results. It will also help you recognize that others may be rejecting your ideas not because of the ideas, but because of the style of delivery.

How We Do What We Do

Interaction style addresses our styles of interacting with others—how we try to influence them and relate to them. It often determines whether we listen to someone or not and whether we like someone.

Unconscious BLM

A man was in the hospital and told his wife that one of his nurses was terrible and one was really good. Being a nurse herself, she had observed them both and thought they had excellent clinical skills and were giving him very good care. Knowing about interaction style differences, she quickly identified that the "terrible" nurse had a style quite opposite to her husband's style and the "good" nurse's style matched her husband's style.

Unconscious BLT

A chief executive has a rather casual, inspiring style, which we call "Get-Things-Going." At first, one of his vice-presidents thought he, too, had the same style, yet his behavior was much more like the "In-Charge" style. When they learned about their interaction style differences, they had a good laugh and the vice-president discovered renewed energy and enthusiasm for his job since he didn't have to suppress his natural style the way he had thought he needed to.

Stress

A manager was constantly frustrated by his boss's "lack of decision making." On discovering his boss had a "Behind-the-Scenes" style and he had an "In-Charge" style, he realized why he had been having a recurring nightmare of trying to drive a car from the passenger side without access to the controls. Understanding the source of the stress allowed him to release himself from the self-imposed responsibility for accomplishing a result that hadn't been defined yet and to give his boss a chance to make the integrative decisions natural to her style.

> *"To understand himself man needs to be understood by another. To be understood by another, he needs to understand the other."*
> —Thomas Hora

Turn the pages to discover your natural interaction style so you too can be released from BLM and BLT and better manage the stress in your life.

Coming to Know Your "Self"

History of the Four Interaction Style Patterns

Throughout the ages, observers of human behavior have repeatedly identified patterns or configurations of behavior. Such holistic sorting of behavior patterns has been recorded for at least twenty-five centuries. Ancient philosophers described four dispositions called temperaments—a choleric, a phlegmatic, a melancholic, and a sanguine. Interpretations of these patterns have varied over the years, with two distinct interpretations, one is David Keirsey's temperament theory and the other relates to the Interaction Style Model.

Most twentieth-century psychologists abandoned holistic observation of human behavior for a microscopic examination of parts, fragments, traits, and so on. To them, all human beings were basically alike—and individual differences were due to chance or conditioning—yet many of them ultimately described patterns that resemble our holistic view.

The seeds were sown for the Interaction Style Model in the 1920s. In 1928, William Marston wrote about the emotional basis for our behavior. John Geier built on Marston's work and developed the DiSC® instrument. Geier looked at traits and clusters of traits that would help us understand how we behave in the "social field." Then came a long string of frameworks and instruments that described the social styles of people. These frameworks yielded descriptions similar to Geier's interpretation of Marston's work.

Many of these authors (see table to left) referenced the work of Carl Jung, Isabel Myers, and Katharine Briggs. Their primary focus, in contrast to Jung, was on outer behavior, not inner states. Some even reference Keirsey's temperament theory. They seemed to not realize they were referencing separate models.

All of these models suggest that these styles or types are inborn. In the meantime, studies continue to be conducted on the various "temperamental" traits that can be identified and tracked over time with physiological measures. Many of these traits seem to relate to the Interaction Styles patterns. Now, how do you find out which pattern fits you? There are several methods.

Personality Instruments

Sometimes people come to understand who they are through self-reporting on personality instruments. No instruments that rely solely on self-reporting are completely accurate. They must all be accompanied by a validation process, preferably involving self-discovery. Many instruments have standards that require face-to-face facilitated feedback with a qualified professional. This booklet is not meant to replace this valuable interactive process but to support it.

Personality instruments that are well researched and well designed can help us tune in to key aspects of who we are. They are designed to reveal ourselves to ourselves. The Myers-Briggs Type Indicator® (MBTI®) has been used to suggest one's Interaction Style, but it is based on the work of Carl Jung and not on the Interaction Style Model. (See Appendix A for more information about the relationship.)

As you read this booklet, allow yourself to try on all four Interaction Style patterns to see which one fits you the best. If you have had exposure to instruments like the MBTI or DiSC, set aside any assumptions about what might be your best-fit Interaction Style™ pattern. While the MBTI is often accurate, it may not be so on all four letters of the type code and the DiSC instrument is based on different testing assumptions. Many who have read the interaction style descriptions have found their styles accurately represented by the four Interaction Style patterns, although these patterns might not match the predicted MBTI or DiSC results. When people really look at the true meaning of the MBTI four-letter code or full DiSC patterns, they find that the letters corresponding to their interaction styles are indeed the better fit. This is why we recommend the use of a self-discovery process—with or without a personality instrument.

Historical References to Four Patterns of Human Interaction

		Directing *(Berens)* Directive *(Keirsey)* Low Responsiveness *(Geier)*	Informing *(Berens)* Informative *(Keirsey)* High Responsiveness *(Geier)*
Responding *(Berens)* **Low Assertiveness**	**Marston/Geier** **DiSC® (Current)** **Social Styles** **Alessandra** **Thomas-Kilman** **Conflict Mode** **Berens**	Compliance/Competence Conscientiousness Analytical Thinker Avoiding Chart-the-Course	Submissive/Steadfastness Steadiness Amiable Relater Accommodating Behind-the-Scenes
Initiating *(Berens)* **High Assertiveness**	**Marston/Geier** **DiSC® (Current)** **Social Styles** **Alessandra** **Thomas-Kilman** **Conflict Mode** **Berens**	Dominance/Directness Dominance Driver Director Competing In-Charge	Inducement/People Focus Influence Expressive Socializer Collaborating Get-Things-Going

Self-Discovery

One powerful way to find your best-fit interaction style pattern is through self-discovery. In this ongoing process, you learn about the four patterns while reflecting on which is most like you. This works very well for many people.

Self-Reflection

The Johari Window*, originally used for improving communication, is a useful map to help us understand this self-discovery process.

The Johari Window

	Known to Self	Unknown to Self
Known to Others	Public Knowledge . . . *What I Show You*	Feedback . . . *Your Gift to Me*
Unknown to Others	Private . . . *Mine to Share*	Unconscious . . . *Not to Probe but I Can Become More Aware and Choose to Share*

For example, there is "Public Knowledge"—aspects we know about ourselves and that are known to others around us. These public aspects of ourselves are easily recognized. What do we talk about over coffee or around the water cooler? Discovering how we communicate in general is one part of getting in touch with who we really are. Listen to what you say and how you say it. What are the kinds of subjects you like to talk about? These topics will likely reflect your natural self. Be aware that your public self may reflect adaptive or learned behavior. This adaptive self is also part of who you are but may not hold the key to what energizes you.

Interaction with Others— Sharing and Feedback

We also learn who we are through our interactions with others. Finding people who are similar to us and comparing notes and sharing stories help many find their own best-fit interaction style pattern. This process often happens in workshops when people openly discuss their interaction styles in order to better understand themselves and others. Sometimes this kind of discussion takes us into the "Private" area of the Johari Window—those aspects known to ourselves and not known to others. In the same way, self-discovery often sends us to this area, at least privately.

One valuable way of finding out who we are is by actively seeking feedback—asking others to tell us how they see us. These people may be trained facilitators or merely people who know us well. The "Feedback" area of the Johari Window gives us the opportunity to learn about those aspects of ourselves unknown to us but known to others. This provides additional information as we explore who we are. And remember, this feedback is a gift, often given through the perspective of the giver—so seek feedback from many people.

Openness to New Information

During the self-discovery process, we sometimes have "Unconscious" information come into our minds—aspects previously unknown to ourselves and unknown to others. In the interaction style model, the unconscious is often where we "store" information about how to "be" in the world. As you explore who you are, stay open to valuable insights from this area.

Many variables may affect your self-discovery process. Be aware that family, social, cultural, and other influences will affect how you view yourself in relation to the interaction style patterns. These influences are often unconscious until they somehow come into our awareness when they are described and pointed out. Stay open and searching. Seek input from all areas of the Johari Window.

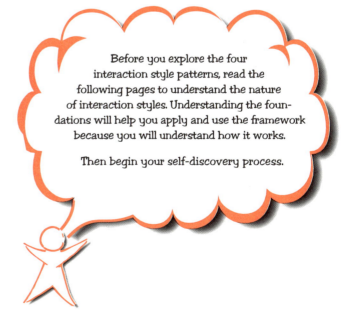

Before you explore the four interaction style patterns, read the following pages to understand the nature of interaction styles. Understanding the foundations will help you apply and use the framework because you will understand how it works.

Then begin your self-discovery process.

---

*Originally formulated by Joseph Luft and Harry Ingham in "The Johari Window: A Graphic Model of Awareness in Interpersonal Relations," in *Group Process: An Introduction to Group Dynamics*, Joseph Luft (Palo Alto, Calif.: National Press Books, 1963), 10–12.

The Nature of Interaction Styles

Interaction Style Is Inborn

From an individual's earliest moments of existence, interaction style patterns can be observed over and over again. These tendencies have been studied and tracked in many individuals over the course of their lifetimes.

> Just as the blueprint for an oak or a pine tree is present in its very seed, so is the Interaction Style pattern present at birth. Differences between two kinds of saplings may appear minute, but close examination will always reveal that the pine sapling is a pine and not an oak. Each is a variety of tree, but the two are organized differently right from the beginning.

> **REMEMBER**
>
> A number of theories describe one's "temperament" or inborn predispositions. The interaction styles model presented here derives from communication theory and biologically based theories of predisposition. This theory is distinct from David Keirsey's Temperament Theory, (see *Understanding Yourself and Others®: An Introduction to Temperament*) yet it follows the same organismic principles.

Understanding your interaction style pattern helps reveal how you are naturally organized—from the beginning.

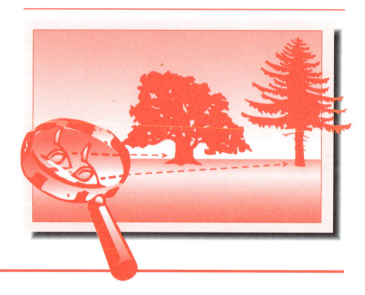

Interaction Style Remains Constant

Our pattern of organization exists from the beginning and influences growth and development. Our interaction style is expressed throughout our life. It is not merely a result of acquiring individual traits from our experiences. Rather, it is a constant internal drive to interact with others in certain ways.

> Just as an acorn will become only an oak and a pine nut will yield only a pine, so one's temperament remains the same from birth. The final type of tree is never "up for grabs" depending on what is "in" this season or available, nor can one "reorganize" an oak—an oak is an oak is an oak!

As we grow and develop, our interaction style pattern stays the same while we evolve into a more mature version of what we were in the beginning.

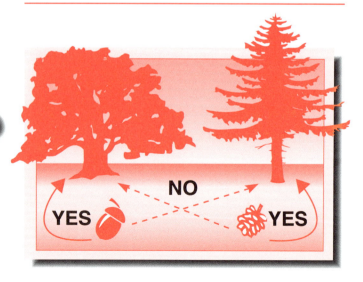

The Nature of Interaction Styles

Interaction Style Drives Behavior

Our behaviors cluster into activity patterns. These activity patterns organize around themes of drives, aims, core beliefs, and fears specific to each Interaction Style. When situations require us to adapt to environments and use behaviors inconsistent with our fundamental nature, our Interaction Style influences that adaptation as well.

> Just as the kind of tree provides the expression of "treeness," the Interaction Style pattern provides the expression of "humanness." Basic "treeness" determines the presence of roots, trunk, and branches and is, in turn, unexplainable without them. "Oakness" or "pineness" determines the form—the shape of the leaves, the size of the trunk, the root system, and all the other characteristics that make the tree "behave" like an oak rather than a pine or any other kind of tree.

Our interaction style influences the pattern of growth and development of character.

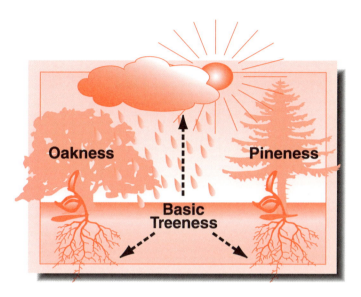

Interaction Style Is Dynamic, Not Static; Influencing, Not Limiting

Interaction Style is a dynamic pattern, always open to influence from the environment. We come into the world with a predisposition, our true self, but growth does not stop with the predisposition. We are free to behave and develop in other ways. We can and do behave in situations in a variety of ways; this is our contextual self.

Consider roles, for example. Our Interaction Style pattern will influence which roles we are drawn to take with others and which ones we fulfill more easily. However, we can and do take roles that go with any Interaction Style in a given situation, and over time they become an aspect of our developed self.

Neither the developed self nor the true self determines what to do in a given situation. That is the role of our contextual self—to act according to the needs of the moment, choosing whether or not to be responsive to the influences of the true self and developed self.

Interaction Style influences growth, variation, and adaptation.

> Use the activities and descriptions that follow to find the pattern of your Interaction Style. Once you experience the certainty of that pattern, you'll find adapting and growing easier and more rewarding.

The Nature of Interaction Styles

Interaction Style Is a Pattern

Even though some of the evidence for the existence of the Interaction Style patterns comes from measurement of physiological traits, Interaction Style is best viewed as a whole pattern, not a cluster of traits. The pattern derives from neurophysiological tendencies.

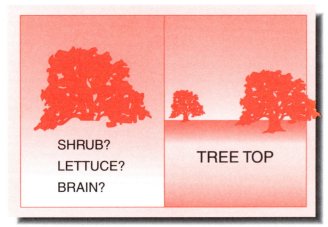

Regardless of your best-fit Interaction Style pattern, you are likely to display some of the characteristics of other styles. On the whole, you are likely to find more of the descriptors of one style pattern than another fitting you. Those characteristics that do fit will more likely occur in response to a specific context rather than being the energy pattern that has been constant over your lifetime. For example, all people want to get a good result, yet only one Interaction Style has getting the best result possible as a driving force in its style of interactions. People frequently choose ways of interacting that fit the overall pattern of their natural organization.

Interaction Style Is Organic

We seem to have a motoric predisposition to react to stimuli in certain ways. For example, some people respond quite actively and others respond in a more relaxed manner. These predispositions give us a tendency to take different stances in relation to others.

Interaction Style is reflective of our "position" or "role" in the communication.

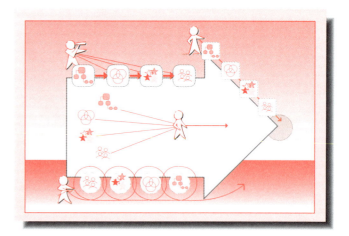

Interaction Style Is A Communication

These stances influence our points of view in any given situation. Our Interaction Style becomes a communication in and of itself. Communication theorists point out that all behavior is communication. In fact it is impossible to not communicate. Even silence sends a message. The meaning of that message is interpreted through the lenses of the receiver who observes various postures and facial expressions. Thus Interaction Style is an important aspect of communication that involves influencing others.

All behavior is communication.

All communication has both a content aspect that conveys the information and a command aspect that influences the receiver of the communication.

Exploring Your Interaction Style

Using Your Experiences

> **REMEMBER**
> Interpret "role" broadly. It may be an assigned role, like chair or facilitator, a relationship role like parent or child or boss, or a role you naturally fall into in an unstructured situation.
>
> Describe whatever comes to your mind as most meaningful to you, not a set definition.

Consider several projects you have worked on in a group. Then answer the following questions in light of those projects.

What role did you usually fall into naturally? What was satisfying about that role? What made it easy?

If you had an assigned role that was uncomfortable, what about the role drained your energy?

When you disagreed with an idea or an approach or when others disagreed with the approach you wanted, how did you try to influence them?

Where did you position yourself in relation to the group?

What did you say or do?

To identify interaction style themes in the above experiences, read the following interaction style characteristics and see which of the four most closely matches your most comfortable style. Then see pages 10-17 to find a good fit for your natural interaction style.

Understanding Yourself and Others®: An Introduction to Interaction Styles

Exploring Your Interaction Style

Chart-the-Course

- Have a course of action in mind beforehand.
- Create a plan (or several workable plans).
- Keep the group on track, allowing for digressions as long as progress is being made.
- Devise, define, describe, or reveal the way to achieve the vision.
- Make deliberate decisions, checking against an already-thought-out process.
- Focus on giving guidance and illumination so the right decision is made.
- Analyze and figure out what needs to be done.
- Plan agendas for project completion and meetings.
- Conceptualize a desired result and how to get there.
  - Foresee how people will respond and plan accordingly.

Behind-the-Scenes

- Do what it takes to get the best result possible.
- See value in contributions from many people or information sources.
- Support the group's process by allowing for digressions then refocusing on the desired outcome.
- Reconcile many voices in communication of the vision.
- Make consultative decisions, integrating many sources of input.
- Focus on understanding the process to get a high quality outcome.
- Aim to produce the best products and results.
- Support others as they do their work.
- Define specifications to meet standards and apply principles.
  - Clarify values and intentions.

In-Charge

- Get things accomplished (often through people).
- Take rapid action to get things done and move on to the next project.
- Lead the group to the goal.
- Articulate the vision and create an environment to achieve it.
- Make quick decisions with confidence in what is needed.
- Focus on getting desired results as soon as possible.
- Execute actions, work all the angles, and remove obstacles.
- Supervise others and provide resources.
- Marshal and mobilize the people, and financial and material resources.
  - Mentor people, finding the talent and nurturing the talent to get the job done.

Get-Things-Going

- Get everyone involved participating.
- Move the group to action along their paths.
- Facilitate the group's process to work with people where they are to get them to where they are going.
- Get the energy moving toward an emerging vision.
- Make enthusiastic, collaborative decisions that ensure buy-in.
- Focus on interactions to get more from the group than group members can get individually.
- Explore options that keep things moving along.
- Make preparations to make things easy for others.
- Discover new ways of seeing things and doing things.
  - Share insights about what something means and what is really going on.

Exploring Your Interaction Style

What Fits?

On the following pages you will find a self-portrait and a more detailed portrait for each of the four interaction style patterns to "try on." As you read through the following four interaction style pattern descriptions, reflect on your group/team experiences from page 7 and the role descriptions on page 8. Use this worksheet to write down words or phrases that fit you as well as people you know.

Chart-the-Course Interaction Style

What fits me...

People I know...

Behind-the-Scenes Interaction Style

What fits me...

People I know...

In-Charge Interaction Style

What fits me...

People I know...

Get-Things-Going Interaction Style

What fits me...

People I know...

REMEMBER

As you read the self-portraits, remember these are written in the language of the style, so pay attention to how comfortable the words feel. Are they things you would say and how you would say them? Ask others who know you well to read the portraits that you think fit you the best. Sometimes others can see our interaction styles better than we can.

Separate the roles you have from the style name. You can be literally In-Charge in a group, and do it with a Behind-the-Scenes style just as you can be working Behind-the-Scenes with an In-Charge style. Which is your natural style, not your role?

Understanding Yourself and Others®: An Introduction to Interaction Styles

Behind-the-Scenes Interaction Style

SELF-PORTRAIT

What most people don't see or appreciate about me is how I get things done. I discover how things relate and add value to each other. I can pull stuff all together to make a better idea or product. When working with someone, I get to know and understand what they're doing, and go about getting the gist of what they want. Then I can stick to their theme or goals, getting to the way it can actually be done and cleaning it up. I have a pretty good capacity to take differing points of view and ask questions to help people see the common ground. Then people can come to a decision about something where they thought they had a lot of differences. I enjoy listening to people, hearing stories and ideas and learning where a person or their ideas are coming from and what their background is. If I'm comfortable, I can ask a lot of questions. I love to banter back and forth and I like adding to or building upon others' stuff.

It takes a lot to truly upset me. When I get upset I usually get very quiet. I want others to understand, but often they don't pick up on it because it's not an external reaction. I am probably one of those people you rarely see angry and I am a very patient and understanding person, but there are limits. If I have not had success at getting my point across, and I keep having to stuff things down, then anger will come out; it's best to leave me alone and let me cool off. Sometimes I feel so frustrated in trying to communicate something that seems so real and important to me, but I am unable to find the right words. This gets even worse when others don't give me time to integrate everything.

Sometimes I avoid conflict at the risk of really doing what would be the best thing to do. I wouldn't do anything that would willfully or consciously hurt someone's feelings. If I'm unhappy about something, I think I basically analyze everything to death. I struggle with myself—how can I be fair, sort through the issues, and balance the needs without being taken advantage of? I have to go sit and figure out in my mind the best way to approach the problem. I can go into a depression and focus on the negative and keep tearing myself to pieces. I like approval from colleagues or family in the sense that I want them to feel comfortable around me and respond well to me.

I don't approve of performance done in bad faith. I feel I work really hard, and I absolutely can't stand somebody not doing their best job. If it's not doing me any harm I will ignore it. I put up with it for a while hoping for a change for the better on its own. If after a reasonable period of being patient, or if it's to the point where I can't go anywhere unless it gets resolved, then I will go the other way and feel a strong need to confront it head on, jumping in to take care of it, or removing my involvement. But this takes me a long time because I will go miles out of my way to avoid it.

I like a well-executed piece of work and I don't do projects haphazardly or halfheartedly. I carry through with my commitments unless I feel hassled or pressured. I like flexibility and am generally accommodating. I prefer to think things through so wasting time and resources can be avoided for the most part. Major decisions can take me forever to decide. I'm very methodical as I try to put everything together. It's as if I try to consider and satisfy every point of view, and I'm not a "fools rush in" kind of person. Unfortunately, I often feel rushed to accomplish something because I have spent too much time on the details. I gather information and get a feel for things, and I need feedback that has a positive impact. I am always trying to understand and go with the flow of things as they are.

I enjoy helping someone solve a problem they've been working on, by understanding them and then helping them discover what will help to overcome the problem—how to deal with it, what tools are needed, or where to go. When it's important, I think I have the patience and an awareness of how to work with people who have areas in which they are limited. I tend to be an encourager of others. If a person has a plan that makes sense to them and seems reasonable to me then I'll support the person in it.

I won't give things to others that I wouldn't be willing to do myself and I don't like asking others to do things for me. I want things done a certain way and don't want to intrude on others' time and space. If I don't think it's really important, I let it sit, put it out of my mind, and forget about it. Whether I agree or not about something has a huge impact on my willingness to follow through, although I will do it eventually. I don't like others imposing their values on me, and I need recognition that my contribution is valuable. I'm trying to learn to say no more often, but if it's needed I usually say I'll help, and I find myself over-committed. I feel I'm a somewhat humble person even though I like to hear positive comments—but hearing them is embarrassing. I don't want the focus to be on me per se. I just want to be accepted and respected.

The Behind-the-Scenes Interaction Style

PORTRAIT

Others see the Behind-the-Scenes style as quietly friendly, approachable, and unassuming. People with this style tend to leave open the option to act by giving information about what they are doing, have done, or are going to do, what the idea is, or what the desired behavior is. Their voice, tone, and gestures also communicate an openendedness that leaves others free to decide as they see fit. They prefer to quietly influence and want others to "want" to do something.

In making decisions, they prefer a consultative approach that takes into account the input of others. When pressed to make quick decisions, they can feel pressured into compromising standards, quality, or their values. They instinctively know deciding too quickly may not yield the best result. They want the outcome to meet people's needs and to be of high quality or accuracy.

With their sense of "we're all in this together," they have a tendency to get in and do the work themselves. Their willingness to do it themselves and not just delegate, as well as their consultative approach, makes people want to go along. They search for commonalities, try to satisfy everyone, and try to make a good idea better by linking it with something else. They see value in people's contributions that others don't see, and they try to make sure those contributions are not ignored—they're often the ones who bring the group back to a point someone made earlier. They often quietly encourage the participation of everyone, yet their own contributions are often not heard because of their low-key style of presentation. Others often mistake their quiet style for lack of confidence and self-assuredness or lack of leadership and are often surprised at the inner strength and influence these people can have.

Sometimes it seems as if their best work is invisible. People just don't realize what goes into it. People of this style are mostly satisfied by having their contributions used, but often feel like unsung heroes—working really hard to make something happen while others get the credit. And yet, when given recognition, they are half embarrassed by it.

Their easy going style makes them pretty good listeners. They are usually seen as agreeable and accommodating and others are often surprised at how tenacious they can be. When the situation or others press them to focus too soon and come to closure, they can have trouble communicating the importance of their own viewpoint. They expect their openness to input to be given in return. If not, they try hard to convince people of the value, the goodness, or the rightness of what they see needs to happen. First, they do it quietly, but if it is really important, they'll push harder, getting frustrated when they can't find the words to convey their message. Then, they find it harder to listen and respond to the input they so value. They can easily get down on themselves, which only makes it worse. Others can help by giving them time to finish their sentences and to clarify their thinking without interrupting. They find it quite disruptive when someone else thinks they already know what they are going to say.

Their tendency to quietly support and encourage others can lead them to be a little too adaptable. They can get sidetracked by others' needs and wants and then they put in extra time and effort to get their own work done. Then they experience an internal conflict between their desire to collaborate and their primary drive to get the best outcome. This stress can leave them internally agitated and yet externally more and more quiet and agreeable. They may agree out of conflict avoidance rather than the true commitment they usually seek.

If stressful situations go on too long, they can switch into an angry attacking mode with name calling and blaming. Such outbursts are rare and seem quite out of character. People of this style are generally more patient with others' flaws and so are slow to anger. It takes a lot before they become visibly upset. They tend to get quiet and internalize the anger first. You may recognize something is wrong, but they will likely deny it, except to those very close to them. You can help by listening or by giving them ample time and space to go away and sort things out and then come back to work it out.

People of this style tend to take a conscientious approach. Doing a well-executed piece of work is important. They often believe the only way to do something is in the very best way possible. Often that means reworking, revising, or reconsidering a decision. Others can become quite impatient with this approach, but in the end they value the high quality it produces.

Understanding Yourself and Others®: An Introduction to Interaction Styles

Chart-the-Course Interaction Style

SELF-PORTRAIT

I like to accomplish things, going beyond expectations, and if something interests me I have an incredible ability to focus and stick with it. I'm good at organizing, strategizing, and planning, and I take the time at the beginning or end of each day to try to plan what's going to happen the following day or list what I will do. I have goals, and I always know there is going to be something next. If I don't have goals, some objectives, or long-term projections, then what's the point? I'm particularly excited when I get an insight and can follow through by doing something—how my life will hopefully be made better by the decision and how this will put me in another place or on another level. Always moving forward, never backward. I also know not to be disappointed if I can't achieve the goal and at least I have something to fall back on. And when everything is on track, when I don't have to worry, I enjoy myself—playing freely without a lot hanging over my head. I hate it when I don't know where things are going.

I'm always observing what's going on, asking questions in order to get to know a person or issue, and inside I am continually reworking, weighing, or questioning things. What do I foresee in the future? What led to now? Is there a smoother, more suitable approach? Can this fit life better? One simply utilizes what's appropriate for the occasion to track and tackle a problem, and I just need to figure out the best way to get to the answer. It's relatively easy to have an answer to tell people. I often resist involving someone else in a task or decision if I think I can do it better myself. I am very independent this way.

When I experience information overload, it's absolutely important to get away. Then I will get back to the person or problem, in a while. If something is still a problem I go back inside myself and analyze what may need to be done and do not panic. In preparing for what I think is going to happen, I go over the scenarios of what should and should not be before I have to make a decision so I can be supportive in a positive way to prevent a crisis. I can take a different approach and give it another shot. Frequently, there are times when I am not just giving out an answer, when I really thought something was the right answer at the time, but later when alone I get a different take—that "aha" experience or realization in hindsight.

I help people by observing what's going on and giving guidance and information, often providing a few techniques to keep them moving on, or putting programs, procedures, or structures in place where they might not have existed before. I like to see people come to realizations—an experience that happens in such a way that a teacher lets others come to realize something important that's already figured out. Sometimes it is very black and white—one level to the next - and there really is only one answer, so I want to get them to see that. I want to be sure people leave with good information and knowing that something isn't impossible, to help them do something different than what they were trying to do. I find people amusing, but it's difficult when someone chooses not to take my advice because I don't want to get into that place of "I told you so." I can't change another person. They are their own person and I have to be able to let go.

I prefer that people directly communicate what's really on their minds. It's an integrity issue. If someone has a problem, then he or she should step up and say so in straightforward terms. If it hurts, we can deal with that, but we can't deal with gossip, innuendo, or games, manipulation and self-absorption, or hinting because someone finds it difficult. If I get into a situation where I feel very strongly, and if I can't put my thoughts into words that make sense, or I really don't think we're going to progress, then I'll walk away from conflict rather than deal with it. I simply cut off that relationship, distancing myself to protect myself. I close the doors and move on, never to look back.

I think I am hard to get to know, and people's first impressions of me are probably not indicative of who I am. It's very easy for me to shut myself off and have my private thoughts yet assume other people know what's going on with me. I've often felt like I am on the outside of a circle watching. I watch from a distance for a while to assess a situation, and I don't expose myself all at once. Or sometimes what I try to explain just doesn't seem to get across so I shut down, saying I don't need to expend energy because it's not that important to me anyway. Similarly, if I'm out of character or don't show emotions and facial expressions, then people often don't quite know how to deal with that. Even though I feel I can be warm with people, I'm a very private person and I will not intrude on anybody's privacy. I can also get too intense and serious and wish I could relax more. I also really admire expediency and the ability to have the physical endurance and strength to do things. I prefer to be thought of as professional, intelligent, skilled, fair, and insightful.

The Chart-the-Course Interaction Style

PORTRAIT

Those with a Chart-the-Course style want others to know what the plan is so they often begin their communications by sharing or getting information. They like to enlighten and inform so people make the right decisions. In the absence of a stated agenda or plan of action, they tend to feel frustrated and even fearful until there is one. They believe that only by considering what we want in the future and entering the present with a plan of action will we successfully accomplish our goals. If no progress is being made, then they become more directing, focusing on the tasks and the time it takes to achieve them. They want people to understand where the group (or project) is going and what the process of getting there will look like. This isn't just about defining the goal but also about describing the best process to use to reach the goal. Then as things come up, decisions come easily and quickly, the right actions are taken, and time is not wasted.

They grow frustrated when other people ignore their well thought out, sometimes detailed, plans. Others just don't realize the importance of the course of action they see as needed, how they've already given it a fair amount of consideration, or how sure they are it is the right thing to do. Then they may feel justified in pushing their agenda or moving forward with the plan anyway if they can. If they can't, they'll try to reach a compromise or even comply with the situation just to move things along. However, if they feel strongly enough, they may feel compelled to leave the situation, rather than fight a losing battle. People may see them as less adaptable than they are. Just because they have worked out what to do doesn't mean they can't stray or rework things. In fact, having the course charted helps them be more flexible. Movement toward the goal is more important than any one course of action and they are quite willing to make adjustments to move the process along.

Usually, they like seeing things from many angles and points of view and gather lots of information during the analysis or plan formulation phase. While they tend to be analytical, when the vision, plan, or analysis of a situation comes to them, they are ready to act on it. They are often so sure of the needed course of action they may dismiss more information or exploration as unnecessary detail.

Charting the course requires disengaging somewhat from what is going on in the external world to be open to and sort through internal information. They seem to enjoy observing people more than interacting. They need a lot of reflection time to review things in their minds and to get focused, both before an event and after. Without this, they can become quite stressed, feel frazzled, and need to withdraw. The solitude and sense of moving forward in activities, like long drives, bike rides, and running, create an inner calm where they can recharge. To get them to consider your input, give them the space and time to reflect on it before insisting on an answer. Otherwise, you will just increase their stress and are likely to get an automatic answer.

People of this style are rather reserved, often seen as somewhat intense, distant, or aloof. They can sometimes be critical as they focus internally on analyzing situations and staying on track, as well as possible. Sometimes others misread their contained nature, calling it uncaring. The opposite is true. Their minds are always working so hard to keep moving toward the goal, they can forget to let people know how much they care. Typically, they are not very self-disclosing and the more stress they feel, the more they hold back and don't express their thoughts or feelings. There is an intensity about them because they see the needed course of action and when there is no progress toward that plan, they get tense.

When there is conflict, they may get more quiet or unemotional and objective, waiting until it is over and then resolving it later. This calm demeanor suggests that nothing is wrong. Those who know them well know there is something wrong and yet don't know what it is or what to do. They have a tendency to walk away from the conflict when they can't put their thoughts into words or think of the right thing to say. They abhor situations where there are many innuendoes to attend to. In situations they can't escape, they can get quite terse, or even rigid, rather than being their usual cooperative selves. You can help them using calm, direct communication indicating you care.

The Chart-the-Course style has a strong focus on productivity, quality, and accomplishment. People with this style like having and giving others the tools to accomplish what is needed so they can do things right and not have to rework them. They want to help in any way they can to improve things. They want feedback, one-on-one or written, seldom in public or with fanfare. Sometimes they want reassurance that they are on course, doing the right thing, and having an impact.

Understanding Yourself and Others®: An Introduction to Interaction Styles

The Get-Things-Going Interaction Style

Get-Things-Going Interaction Style

SELF-PORTRAIT

I'm sort of a playful catalyst. I'm at my best when I meet someone who has an interesting idea, talent, or project. Then I start aligning with that person—I sort of feel them out—and sometimes I see the great idea that's there. Or the questions they ask shed light on something about which I have a great idea. The feedback I get is that I have a way of bringing everything together and delivering it back to people in a concise way, with a spirit of cooperation. People are probably in many ways the most important part of my life. It makes me feel really good when people notice something noteworthy about me, when people like and respect me. What I don't like is being "average."

I am described as someone people can come to when they want an idea or help with a problem they're trying to solve. I'm a good listener and have the ability to empathize in the sense that my focus is sharing information, ideas, and coaching, and not simply giving specific advice. Giving directions is boring. What's fun is watching light bulbs go off and the excitement of learning, to teach and help people see what they can do. I like to know at the end of the day that people are walking around with something new and better for life and that I helped. I help the person perceive how things are going on, and I can give information that feeds into what he or she freely wants, which seems right. I do not put any demands on people. I provide encouragement and support to let them know I think they can do it. They may leave with or without a specific plan but they leave with knowledge that they are a special person, and they can make a contribution to society. Then I feel great. And if indeed there is a real problem I probably will do something to help straighten it out.

I like things on a casual basis, and people tell me that somehow I capture their attention and I don't even know what I do, except that I am genuinely interested in liking others and their liking me. I need contact: anything that brings connection, hearing other people's stories and telling stories. I love having people around me, because it's fun and doesn't need a lot of elaboration. At work, I want people to participate and get involved without rigidly structuring what's going to happen. If one is authoritarian, then people feel less appreciated. I share my ideas and accept others' ideas and I admire people who can openly share everything and solve the problem right there—they work with people and people work with them. One problem for me has typically been being too friendly and open. It's as if I don't know how to not be out in the forefront. I can give forth an image of comfort and ease when that's really not the case.

Sometimes I offend people, yet it's difficult for me to interpret why. I see people's needs, I tell them, and maybe they're not ready, or I support where they're coming from even though that can be disruptive to others. I usually come from a well-meaning place—I want everyone to be happy and get along—and I try to facilitate or act as a go-between, but sometimes it just doesn't work out. Certain aspects of solving a problem sometimes mean stepping on people's toes, and that's difficult because I want things to be smooth. It makes me crazy if I'm in conflict with someone who wants to walk away. When I hear a person's confrontational tone it's like I'm curling up inside myself. So many times I tend to skirt the real issue. I tend to be sensitive, and on a certain level I need approval, but in a different way I don't need any approval at all.

I have a passion and intensity about life. I have a wide range of interests, tend to jump into things, and am often frustrated that there doesn't seem to be enough time to pursue all that interests me. I like to think I always look for the good or humor in a situation or I look for a way to change the situation. I can become a pretty strong advocate with a really high energy level in terms of getting involved and getting things done. In fact, I tend to over-extend; I'm busy from the time I get up to the time I go to bed, and I very rarely have nothing to do. If I'm under a lot of stress, I tend to think people are looking at me in a negative way. Then I may panic under the pressure, running in circles and misinterpreting a lot of things that I find out later were not the case. When things are terrible, I close up and don't talk. And when I'm really depressed, I will start thinking about all the bad things that have happened.

My goal in life is to enjoy myself and make sure other people get some sense of how important it is to enjoy and seek something in life. You've got to have some incentive in order to get up every morning and go. I'm thrilled to meet interesting new people and I love to explore the world. I guess I appear to be very lucky but a lot of times that just comes from being open and observant on my part. I see myself as a facilitator of people's processes and problems, probing and pushing, feeding back what I hear so I can hold on to what they're talking about, what they really mean. Knowing that I am a positive influence is a driving force in my life.

The Get-Things-Going Interaction Style

PORTRAIT

People of this style do a lot to Get-Things-Going. To get people interested, they may give them a lot of information. They like making it possible for people to do more together than they can do individually. Sometimes they just go ahead and do things that will make it easier for others without being asked. They know people will do better work if they really buy in, so they like to present many ideas and see where people take them. They realize that they make more suggestions than any one person can follow, but they can get discouraged if they get no feedback. One of their biggest frustrations is when people aren't responding—doing something productive, brainstorming, or just getting involved. Then they can get frustrated, fidgety, or bored. In fact, the interchange they seek may be just what is needed to get things moving along.

Although they may not see themselves this way, people of this style are often so assertive in their informing way that people feel like they just have to go along with whatever is put forth. Most people see them as energetic, with an animated style and flowing gestures that engage people. They tend to be passionate and intense and really like to get others excited about something. They often have trouble choosing which path to follow since they find so many exciting and interesting things to do and have so many ideas. Others sometimes see them as scattered, and their idea generation can feel like a whirlwind. Sometimes they make snap decisions they later rethink, seeming somewhat impulsive. However, often those decisions are just right and become a turning point in their lives or shift the energy of a group.

They are often at their best at the beginning of something when they have the most energy and enthusiasm—trying to get people going with enough motivation to be able to carry on alone. People often notice they get more done or have more ideas when working with people of this style. And they make things fun. Yet sometimes they can tire of always having to be the upbeat and energetic ones, and the motivator role becomes a burden instead of a joy.

People of this style often find themselves liked and trusted. They have a genuine interest in people—learning about them and where they come from. Travel often satisfies their desire to learn—about people, cultures, and ways of thinking.

They tend to be persuasively expressive of thoughts and feelings, often attracting attention and inspiring people to go along. They usually like being the focus of attention and in the center of conversations. Their enthusiastic energy becomes contagious, often getting others to express themselves too. Sometimes their expressiveness shows up in forthrightness—"telling it like it is." They do not mean to be rude and are often surprised when others are offended.

They tend to be good at finding out what others are needing or wanting. They listen, ask questions, and then give information back to help the person see more clearly what they need. Often they go to great lengths to help the person meet those needs or get what they want. Teaching of any kind is one of the ways they help. They love the experience of learning and tend to view life as a constant, emergent process of teaching and learning.

People of this style prefer to stay engaged in friendly interaction. They try very hard to meet the expectations of others and would prefer to avoid conflict. They want relationships to go smoothly, with no tension. As with their other interactions, they prefer an exploratory approach where information is freely shared, its meanings explored and problems unraveled. When others speak to them with a confrontational tone, they want to withdraw. Yet they also want to work through the conflict so they can get on with the relating.

They prefer to talk things out and they feel particularly stressed when others don't want to interact. Then they can get a sort of panicky feeling, which leads them to turn up the volume on their expressiveness. This can become an angry, blaming attack as the situation worsens. But once expressed, their anger is usually over, especially if they were able to re-engage and interact productively. If the stress worsens, they close up, don't talk, and just go along. It helps to get involved with them in their other interests.

People of this style often use humor to break the ice as well as stories, metaphors, and analogies to warm up the interaction and lighten the moment. These stories help people relate. Their stories also help make things clearer so people can understand each other and communicate more easily. Sometimes they may feel like stories are the only way for people to really hear what's being said. More task-oriented folk experience this storytelling as a distraction, especially when there is work to do and little time. Others just don't realize how much work gets done because of this catalytic and facilitative style.

The In-Charge Interaction Style

In-Charge Interaction Style

SELF-PORTRAIT

I always want to be doing something more, and I've been able to handle responsibilities since a fairly early age. If things are out of control, that drives me crazy, but that doesn't mean I have to be the one In-Charge. I need to be organized, with some leadership in place. However, not organizing, not problem solving, and not leading is hard for me. If there's a problem, then it needs to be resolved. It's easy to get upset, wondering why something isn't already taken care of. When I think a solution is there, I'm impatient with a problem lingering on and on. Backtracking does not feel good to me either unless I'm trying to think of ways to make improvements. The main thing is to focus my concentration on something. There is this feeling of responsibility and enjoyment to help make a difference or get something accomplished. I will take on something and move it along just to have met some goals! I like to have control over my own life—personal and professional. My life does not just evolve; I make it happen.

I enjoy having the answers that will help others. I have a relative easiness dealing with people, in the sense that I am interested in a lot of things, and I am constantly being asked to give my opinion of others and their situations. I like to work with others to improve their behavior and improve productivity and quality of life, and I have a sense of resource availability. I know who needs what and who has what to offer, and I do a lot of linking people and resources. Getting things done with a group of people is what it's all about, and I will make decisions based on the good of the group, the family, whatever. I think this requires a willingness to make tough decisions, work hard, and be straight with people. I will see the solution relatively quickly, and maybe 90 percent of the time my solutions have been effective for them. One of my problems is listening, in the sense that I have probably already thought things through before we even got to the point we're at. I really make an effort to not come off as dogmatic.

Communication is a major piece of my life. I am pretty forward with how I think, and I try to be nice but I don't beat around the bush when talking to people. Integrity means that you keep your word. And I don't carry grudges or endorse preferential treatment. In fact, I don't feel I'm always liked. I love to laugh and I like humor where people feel more comfortable and are enjoying one another's fun. At the same time, others say I do not suffer fools gladly.

If someone is trying to take advantage of me, I very much let him or her know about it. It's easy to get irritated quickly about a behavior or a situation, but I can put it quickly aside. If I'm really upset, I'll let myself calm down, figure out what I'm going to say, and confront the situation, showing them what they've done wrong. I don't like it when something—or someone—is not given the care and attention deserved and I get frustrated when people don't work hard or try to undermine me. Typically, things don't rattle me, and when they do, it takes a lot and only lasts a short period because we can go on. My response to making mistakes is, did you learn anything from it? If we could all just deal with people face to face, we would have a much better world.

I work quickly with the big picture in mind. I anticipate, plan in advance, prepare, and make suggestions. I enlist others to do the follow-through, and I'm on to completing the next idea. Then I come back for closure, because I want to be there when credit or reward is given and to see the result. I like being appreciated for effort or the job well done. I am a person who wants others to pay attention, to listen, and accept my ideas, but I have to watch that my plans don't become something that I just drop everyone into or make everyone conform to. I wish I could balance work and life a little better. I relax when I'm ahead of things.

I love the challenge of taking chaos and creating order, something pleasing. I have very high expectations and expect some kind of perfection out of other people and myself. I like to look good. I've always been confident that nothing is ever completely broken. It can be figured out and fixed or remade to get the job done or situation resolved. If the mission or whatever it is, is over there, throw any obstacle my way and I'll find a way around it. I really believe anyone can do anything if one sets his or her mind to it—maybe not exceptionally well, but it can be done. What usually sets the boundary for me is if I am willing to pay the price. I admire people who have been through something and moved beyond it. I have tremendous energy and staying power, and I've directed that toward succeeding at many causes and goals. I am typically handling several things at one time. What's satisfying is people saying to me at the end of the day that they don't know how I do it.

The In-Charge Interaction Style

PORTRAIT

The In-Charge style's presence and sense of composure gives others a sense of confidence that "This person knows what they are doing. They have it all together." This confidence is conveyed nonverbally in the way the person moves, the pace of speech, and tone of voice. With some, their voice just wraps around you and you feel drawn into action. With others of this style, their voice conveys a commanding quality that leaves little room for objection. The more chaotic a situation, the more commanding and in control they appear. People seem to assume they know where to go and what to do and they wind up leading even if they didn't intend to or want to. Others of this style like the attention that comes with leadership and accomplishment. They may not recognize they like it, but they do enjoy having the answers and being in a position to help improve productivity and the quality of peoples' lives.

They want to set the tone, the standards, and the values that influence the outcomes. They want a strong say in running their relationships so things are done the right way. They accomplish things through others and often communicate with directives that tell others what to do and by when. Delegating usually comes easily. They prefer communication to be straightforward and to the point, dealing with conflict directly and expressing what they think and feel. If they overdirect, they can seem bossy and overbearing. Being direct with them shows the same confidence they exude. However, telling them what to do usually insults them.

People of this style tend to set very high standards, sometimes expecting perfection. They focus on achievement and a constant quest to be better. When they (and others) do not perform at the high level expected, they are likely to be disappointed and critical. On the other hand, these expectations often help others rise to meet the high standards. In high-task situations, many mistake the achievement and accomplishment orientation of the In-Charge style for an absence of caring. However, they often show they care by making sure people get the resources they need and they are often masterful at linking people with resources and removing both tangible and intangible obstacles to their performance. They love helping people achieve.

When there are obstacles, they accept them as challenges. They tend to believe that anything is possible if you just set your mind to it. In fact, they love a challenge and really admire people who have been through something difficult and have moved beyond it. In the face of adversity, their bounce-back resilience keeps them going in spite of what might look like a defeat.

They have an awareness of time being short that others don't have and a sense of urgency because they want to accomplish so much. People of this style are usually energetic and fast paced. They want to always be doing something productive and often have a very hard time relaxing and just sitting still, even at home. They tend to be impatient when things are moving too slowly or are not getting done and tend to do many things at once.

People often misunderstand their strong orientation to time and task completion for being controlling. It isn't that they need to control everything, they just need to feel the situation is under control. If they get a sense of things not being under control, they have a tendency to take over or at the least clench their jaws with tension. Sometimes it is hard for them to relax and let events unfold. They find it painful when they can't direct action and they see action is needed. Usually they will find a way to confront the issue.

When they feel out of control, they feel very stressed. Under stress, they might not recognize their increased efforts to control and may become quite autocratic—forcing their action agenda, vision, values, or plans onto others. They usually relate well with people, but in this stressed state they become insensitive and uncaring—sometimes lashing out with blame, maneuvering or bulldozing, and imposing their thoughts and desires onto others. Then they get on with it—no grudges. When controlling doesn't work, they are likely to shift to avoidance tactics to handle their out-of-control feeling. Humor is an important way for them to communicate and deal with some of their frustrations when things aren't being accomplished or everybody is rehashing an issue. You can help by joining in their humor.

Their philosophy is "Nothing ventured, nothing gained." Mistakes are to be learned from. Being decisive, they tend to expect others to make quick decisions and they become impatient when details slow down decisions. When things are undecided and up in the air, they push for decisions. They find it better to decide and not miss the opportunity, and they tend to feel confident they can correct their course if need be. People often look to them for help with decisions.

Understanding Yourself and Others®: An Introduction to Interaction Styles

Clarifying Your Interaction Style

By this point, you may see yourself in some of these patterns. Perhaps you are very clear about which pattern fits you the best. Most often, however, people find themselves in multiple patterns. That is understandable because the patterns are characteristic of abstract categories, and real people are complex living systems with many aspects to them.

This self-discovery process is like shopping for shoes. You want to find the best fit, one that supports you and doesn't cramp you. Use these pages to help you sort out your own particular hierarchy and find which interaction style pattern is really yours. Experience has shown that once people find their true interaction style pattern, they experience a rush of energy and delight in knowing who they are. From that time forward, they can take charge of their lives and make better choices to have their needs met. They can also more easily manage their stress and attract the resources and opportunities they need.

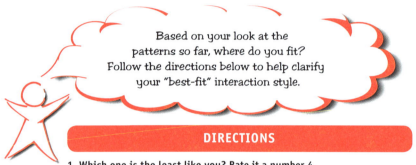

Based on your look at the patterns so far, where do you fit? Follow the directions below to help clarify your "best-fit" interaction style.

DIRECTIONS

1. Which one is the least like you? Rate it a number 4.
2. Then ask yourself, If I had to give up or do without one of the remaining, which one would that be? Rate it a number 3.
3. Use the following three pages to help you sort out which one of the two remaining interaction style patterns is your "best-fit" interaction style.
4. (OPTIONAL) To help you clarify further, have someone who knows you well read the descriptions to help you decide.

Things-in-Common

We often relate to more than one interaction style pattern because each pattern has something in common with the others. These things-in-common reveal themselves in the interactions between people, especially in our communications. As you try to sort out which interaction style is the most natural fit for you, you may identify a preference for one or the other of the dynamics that are at play when people interact. These dynamics are

- Directing versus Informing communications—ways we influence others
- Initiating versus Responding roles—ways to define relationships
- Control versus Movement focus—where we focus our attention when interacting

These dynamics are always operating in a situation, and if we become polarized along these dimensions as we interact with others, miscommunication and misunderstanding are probable and likely to result in destructive conflict. However, we need to remember that we always have at least one aspect in common with someone of a different interaction style.

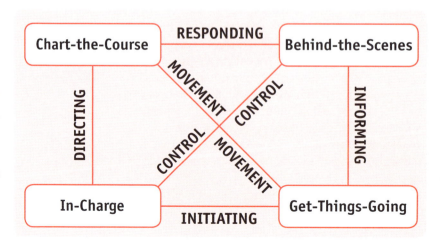

Clarifying Your Interaction Style

Communication—Ways We Influence Others

All communications that involve getting someone else to do something can be classified along a continuum from very directive to very informing. This dynamic involves the style of the communication as well as the words.

Directing

In directive communications, there is a sense of time urgency to get a task done. The focus is on accomplishment of the task. These kinds of communications are most effective when there is little or no choice about getting certain tasks done or in a crisis. Nonverbal and extraverbal aspects often carry the message of an orientation to "time and task" or getting things done with a sense of time urgency.

Informing

In informing communications, there is a desire to motivate to action by giving information. These communications are most effective when people need to be motivated internally and enrolled in the process so they buy in to the goal or the way things are being done. Nonverbal and extra-verbal aspects often carry the message of an orientation to enrolling and engaging others or wanting others to "want to . . . ."

Things-in-Common	**Directing**	**Informing**
Focus On	• Task/time focus	• Process/motivation focus
Intent	• Give structure, direct	• Evoke, draw forth, inspire, seek input
Behavior	• Tell, ask, urge • Non-verbally moving forward, definite	• Inform, inquire, explain, describe • Non-verbally flowing, open, eliciting
Comfort Zone	• Comfortable telling people what to do • Less comfortable giving information and leaving alone	• Comfortable giving information only • Less comfortable telling people what to do
Examples	• "Ask Bob for specific instructions on preparing the report." • "Ellen, would you call some hotels about dates in August for fifty people for a two-day seminar?"	• "Bob has some information that might help you with that report." • "Ellen, do we have information on conference sites for a two-day seminar in August for fifty people?"
Tendencies	• Impatient with emergent process • Often surprised when people resist being told what to do • May be frustrated by lack of a clear position • Tend to act certain that they are right • May be seen as bossy	• More patient with emergent processes • Often surprised when information is not acted on • May be offended at being told what to do • More likely to seem non-commital • May be seen as indecisive

REMEMBER

Separate your assigned roles from your natural interaction style. We can engage in either kinds of behaviors, often flexing according to the needs of the situation. Sometimes we get stuck in our style preference or are blind to the impact of our own natural style on the effectiveness of our communications.

To find your "best-fit" interaction style, ask yourself, "Am I naturally more directing or more informing?" If directing, then Chart-the-Course or In-Charge is probably a better fit. If informing, then Behind-the-Scenes or Get-Things-Going would be a better match.

Understanding Yourself and Others®: An Introduction to Interaction Styles

Clarifying Your Interaction Style

Directing–Informing Continuum

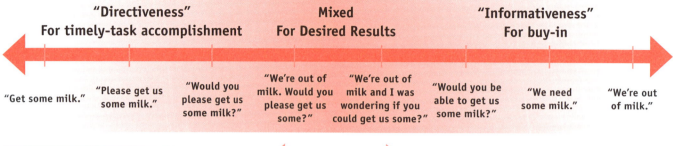

| "Directiveness" For timely-task accomplishment | Mixed For Desired Results | "Informativeness" For buy-in |

"Get some milk." • "Please get us some milk." • "Would you please get us some milk?" • "We're out of milk. Would you please get us some?" • "We're out of milk and I was wondering if you could get us some?" • "Would you be able to get us some milk?" • "We need some milk." • "We're out of milk."

Directing ⇐ ⇒ Informing

Directing
- More forceful tone of voice to communicate urgency
- Often more straightforward statements
- Can imply a one-up/one-down relationship, yet focus may be merely on getting the task done
- Can either seem brusque or polite and friendly
- Moving forward, definite, boundary setting

Informing
- More tentative tone of voice to invite agreement or buy-in
- Often more subtle statements
- Can imply a like-for-like, egalitarian relationship, yet may seem manipulative
- Can either seem wimpy or self-confident and engaging
- Flowing, open, eliciting

The Directing-Informing continuum refers to actual communications. The Directing-Informing dynamic refers to a dichotomous preference for a style of communication.

Relationship Defining Aspects of Communication*

Much of whether a communication is directive or informative is conveyed through the way the message is delivered and the meanings that can be inferred from it. All behavior communicates. All communications have both a report aspect and a command aspect. The report aspect is the content of the communication. The command aspect is the relationship-defining aspect of the communication.

Directive communications often, but not always, imply a relationship definition of "one-up". In other words, if I tell you what to do, I am in some way one-up on you. Boss-subordinate and parent-child relationships often require directive communications because the person In-Charge knows more about the task and holds the responsibility for getting the task done.

Informing communications often, but not always, imply a relationship definition of equality and sometimes of being "one-down." In other words, if I give you some information about something, you are free to act on it as you see fit. The focus is on eliciting input and having the other person truly want to do something or truly see the need to do it. Or it can communicate that you know more or better than I do and I have no power in this situation, so here is some information (thus, I am one-down on you).

Roles often define relationships in and of themselves. Roles like boss, parent, teacher, or supervisor all imply a one-up relationship. When we are in those roles, we may be inclined to use directing communications, or at least think we do. Roles like friend and co-worker imply an equal relationship and our natural style, whether directing or informing, may come through more easily.

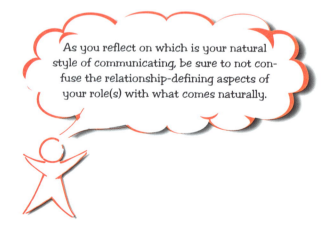

As you reflect on which is your natural style of communicating, be sure to not confuse the relationship-defining aspects of your role(s) with what comes naturally.

---

* For more information about communication theory see *Pragmatics of Human Communication: A Study of Interactional Patterns, Pathologies, and Paradoxes*, Watzlawick, Paul; Janet Helmick Beaven and Don D. Jackson (New York: W.W. Norton and Company, 1967).

Clarifying Your Interaction Style

Roles—Ways to Define Relationships

When we first meet people, we have a choice in setting the pace and tone of the interaction. We can either initiate the interaction or respond with agreement or disagreement to the initiating moves of the other person. This dynamic gives us clues to roles and situations that energize and fatigue us.

Initiating

Those who gravitate toward initiating roles are usually quite comfortable making the first move in a relationship—introducing themselves first or starting a lively conversation. This is often seen as being assertive or one-up. People with a preference for initiating tend to be uncomfortable with long periods of silence or in situations that require them to not engage others in interaction.

Responding

Those who tend to responding roles usually prefer to wait for the other person to make the first move, responding to opening comments by engaging in the conversation or giving minimal response. This is often seen as being reticent or one-down. In reality, the perceived hesitance may be a lack of comfort with defining the relationship for the other person. People with a preference for responding tend to be uncomfortable in situations that require them to start a conversation with a stranger.

Things-in-Common	Initiating	Responding
Focus On	• External world	• Internal world
Intent	• Reach out, interact	• Reach in, reflect
Behavior	• Initiates interactions • Fast pace, active • Extraverting and gregarious	• Responds and reflects • Slow pace, patient • Introverting and solitary
Comfort Zone	• Comfortable making the first move in new relationships • Less comfortable with silence	• Less comfortable initiating new relationships • Comfortable with silence
Examples	• Think out loud. Jump right in with comments. Tend to speak and act, then reflect. • Easier to get to know	• Think before commenting. Tend to reflect or try out something, then speak and act. • Harder to get to know
Tendencies	• Impatient with slow pace • Often surprised when people don't want to talk • May be frustrated by lack of feedback and interaction • May be seen as intrusive	• Pressured by a fast pace • Often surprised when people think they are angry • May be frustrated at lack of reflection time • May be seen as withholding

REMEMBER

This aspect is about role relationships. While this aspect correlates with the widely known personality dimension of Extraversion and Introversion, the Jungian definitions are much broader.

To find your "best-fit" interaction style, ask yourself, "Am I more initiating or more responding?" If initiating, then In-Charge or Get-Things-Going is probably a better fit. If responding, then Behind-the-Scenes or Chart-the-Course would be a better match.

Clarifying Your Interaction Style

Attention—Focus and Interest

In any given interaction, we attend to different aspects. Some people are more focused on controlling some aspect of the interaction. Others are more focused on moving things along.

Control

The In-Charge style and the Behind-the-Scenes style have in common an aim to control the outcome of the interaction or the situation. With the In-Charge style control is sought over the resources, like time and tasks, to get the result as quickly as possible. In the extreme, people of this style may be quite active in seeking control and may have a tendency to "push things through." With the Behind-the-Scenes style, control is sought over the inputs and outputs to get the best result possible. In the extreme, people of this style may "hold it back" until the result is just right or enough input is had.

Movement

The Get-Things-Going style and the Chart-the-Course style have in common an aim to move things along. With the Get-Things-Going style, there is a focus on getting the quickest start and checking in with people along the way. This can be quite an active energetic process, and in the extreme people of this style may "randomize and scatter". With the Chart-the-Course style, the focus is on determining the best action to take and monitoring progress along the way. In the extreme, people of this style may stand back and "overplan" without input and become rigid in following the plan.

Things-in-Common	Control	Movement
Focus On	• Control over the outcome	• Movement toward the goal
Intent	• To get a desired result	• To see progress and action toward the goal
Behavior	• Control information flow • Check against the desired outcome • Ensure the result is achieved	• Create milestones or benchmarks • Check in with the group for progress • Motivate and forge ahead
Comfort Zone	• When they have a measure of control and say so over the outcome	• When they are given the project and told to go ahead with it and then things start moving along
Examples	• "I wish they would just listen to me." • "We need to hold off on that project until we work through the bugs." • "Let's get it done now!"	• "I wish she'd just let me go ahead with it." • "Good, we're making progress." • "Trust the process."
Tendencies	• To get too focused on the outcome and be stubborn about the control	• To get too focused on moving forward and rush to act without considering the result

REMEMBER

Anyone can have control issues regardless of this attention on control. This is not about psychological issues resulting from trauma or coercive environments. It is about influencing through either artistic control or position power.

Using what you have learned, rank the interaction style patterns from 1 to 4, with 1 being your "best-fit" interaction style.

Chart-the-Course
Directing
Responding
Interested in Movement ☐

Behind-the-Scenes
Informing
Responding
Interested in Control ☐

In-Charge
Directing
Initiating
Interested in Control ☐

Get-Things-Going
Informing
Initiating
Interested in Movement ☐

Patterns of Interaction Styles

These four interaction style descriptions are presented on this page in a short and concise way to give you the basic core framework for each interaction style pattern.

The Four Interaction Style Patterns

Chart-the-Course

The theme is having a course of action to follow. People of this style focus on knowing what to do and keeping themselves, the group, or the project on track. They prefer to enter a situation having an idea of what is to happen. They identify a process to accomplish a goal and have a somewhat contained tension as they work to create and monitor a plan. The aim is not the plan itself, but to use it as a guide to move things along toward the goal. Their informed and deliberate decisions are based on analyzing, outlining, conceptualizing or foreseeing what needs to be done.

Behind-the-Scenes

The theme is getting the best result possible. People of this style focus on understanding and working with the process to create a positive outcome. They see value in many contributions and consult outside inputs to make an informed decision. They aim to integrate various information sources and accommodate differing points of view. They approach others with a quiet, calm style that may not show their strong convictions. Producing, sustaining, defining, and clarifying are all ways they support a group's process. They typically have more patience than most with the time it takes to gain support through consensus for a project or to refine the result.

In-Charge

The theme is getting things accomplished through people. People of this style are focused on results, often taking action quickly. They often have a driving energy with an intention to lead a group to the goal. They make decisions quickly to keep themselves and others on task, on target, and on time. They hate wasting time and having to back track. Mentoring, executing actions, supervising, and mobilizing resources are all ways they get things accomplished. They notice right away what is not working in a situation and become painfully aware of what needs to be fixed, healed, or corrected.

Get-Things-Going

The theme is persuading and involving others. They thrive in facilitator or catalyst roles and aim to inspire others to move to action, facilitating the process. Their focus is on interaction, often with an expressive style. They Get-Things-Going with upbeat energy, enthusiasm, or excitement, which can be contagious. Exploring options and possibilities, making preparations, discovering new ideas, and sharing insights are all ways they get people moving along. They want decisions to be participative and enthusiastic, with everyone involved and engaged.

Patterns of Interaction Styles

Each interaction style is a pattern of interrelated characteristics, not merely a cluster of traits. You may find some of the characteristics on each pattern fit you. You may also find some of the characteristics on the graphic of your best-fit interaction style pattern don't fit you, but the overall theme of the pattern fits.

The Graphic Representation

An arrow was chosen to represent the concept of a drive that seems to power our behavior and move us toward certain outcomes rather than others. Inside the arrow are the characteristics that are hidden from view. Outside the arrow are the characteristics that are visible to others and point to the existence of the internal drive.

Drive

A basic psychology textbook defines drive as "The psychological representation of a physiological need; a complex of internal conditions brought about by sensitivity to certain stimuli that impels an organism to seek a goal."* A drive is compelling and it takes energy to resist it.

Core Beliefs

Core beliefs related to the drive seem to be hidden to us as we interact with others. These core beliefs lead us to operate with certain pre-suppositions about how people operate and about what is important. Core beliefs lead us to take certain roles in relation to others in order to influence them.

Aim

Aim refers to the intended outcome of satisfying the drive. It is the goal to which we aspire and seem driven to work toward, covertly as well as overtly.

Attributes

The attributes in front of the arrow indicate the demeanor we have as we interact with others. This is often how others see us and we may not be aware of these attributes. To have a demeanor other than the one that is natural takes effort until it is practiced over and over. Yet, adaptable as we are, we can take on other roles, so demeanors can be misleading.

Talents

The "wheels" are our means for getting to the goal. Each style seems to have a set of talents for getting certain internal drives met.

*Psychology Today, an Introduction. 3rd ed. (New York: Random House, 1975) p 670.

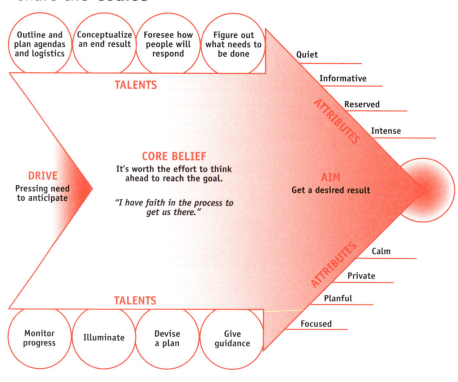

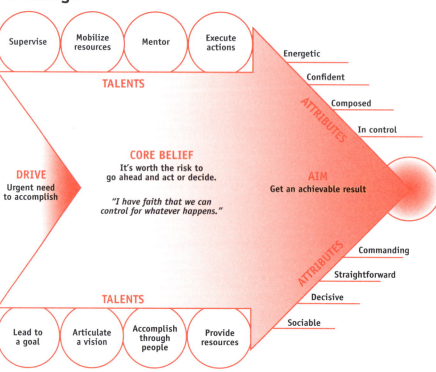

Patterns of Interaction Styles

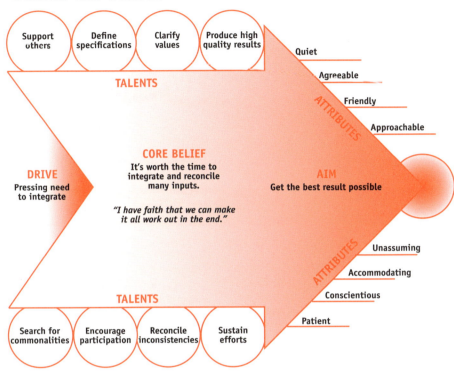

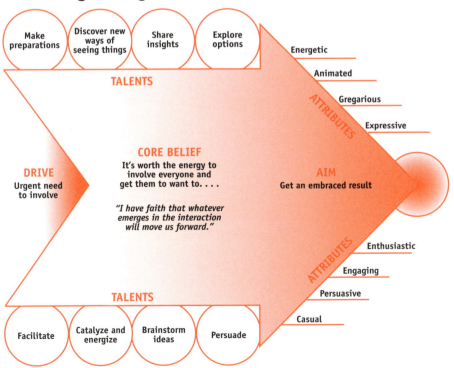

Role Expectations

Role expectations can influence how we see ourselves. Roles are a set of norms applied to social categories such as leadership, gender, and cultures. It is often very hard to step outside our role expectations, especially those from culture, to see our true selves rather than our adapted selves. To find your "true self," you may need to separate from acquired role expectations such as leadership, gender, and culture.

Leadership is behavior that occurs in relationship to other people. Don't assume that if you are not a leader by title, you can't have an In-Charge style. Likewise, don't assume that a natural Behind-the-Scenes style means not being a leader. Leadership involves influencing people and inspiring them to action. Successful leadership can happen using any one of the interaction styles.

Cultural expectations influence how men and women communicate differently. Women seem to use more informing communications and men seem to use more directing communications.* Aspects of culture besides gender make a difference as well. In high-context cultures, where attention is put on the meanings conveyed non-verbally, communications tend to be more generally informing. In low-context cultures, where most meaning is derived from the actual words used, communications tend to be more generally directing. Also, in some cultures, power-distance is an important communication factor. In these cultures, those in roles of authority or status are often seen as more directive than those with lower status and less authority.**

So take some time to sort out the effect these cultural expectations may have on your interaction style. If they are counter to your inborn nature, you may have adapted so well that it may take a bit of observation and sorting through to find your best fit.

---

* *You Just Don't Understand*, Tannen, Deborah., (New York: William Morrow and Company, 1990).

***Culture and Organizations: Software of the Mind*, Hofstede, Geert (New York: McGraw-Hill, 1997).

Identifying Others

Identifying Others*

The examples below of different approaches to the same job illustrate how each style likes to do things differently. Read each description as a whole pattern to see the "whole" style and try not to focus on single words or isolated behavior. Remember, people vary greatly, so a description of a specific person with your interaction style may not match you perfectly.

See if you can identify interaction styles in different settings using what you have learned. In the box provided, write which interaction style you think best fits that description. Look for the answers on page 35.

*The following two pages were modified by Dario Nardi, from his book, *Character and Personality Type: Discovering Your Uniqueness for Career and Relationship Success* (Huntington Beach, Calif: Telos Publications, 1999).

Two Trainers

Marilyn

Marilyn loves stepping out into the group and "joining the people." She gets people thinking and involved in activities, exploring and relating problems. That's a lot of fun and makes it easy to pull the good stuff from the interactions as they happen. Often people catch on extemporaneously right as they're in the thick of things like family. Marilyn feels over-structuring is limiting and creates distance; that's counter to the whole idea of learning.

Madeline

Madeline does training and education, and has conceived of several illuminating group and individual activities and tools, often using software or other mediums. Planning the right set-up and laying out an effective process guides people to jump beyond the analysis and problem-solving skills they already have while respecting the individual. Within a flexible framework, memorable moments and a lot of variety and fun are possible. She trusts her process.

Two Executives

Linda

Linda shepherds her company. Those who work beside her know how involved and dedicated she is behind her calm, easy style and friendly demeanor. She seeks input from many advisors and considers what's important and all the various options to find the right product and the most elegant design with the highest quality. She wants every product to have value and bring in money. Linda finds it easiest to make decisions when everything quickly falls together.

Mike

As soon as he arrives in the office, Mike organizes people to "do the vision." His company brings to customers the resources to achieve a better life, and he also works hard to teach his employees how to succeed. He instills in them qualities like confidence to take the next step, encourages ambition to venture into new areas, and massages the business model to keep growing the business. Mike gets his hands dirty when needed and values humor to overcome tensions.

Two Office Workers

Diana

Diana is her company's interdepartmental liaison. Her most important contributions come in two kinds—developing individual potential by getting people on track and pointing out needs and advising higher management of directions to take for the future for everyone's good, such as reorganizing office space. Though she's always there to help guide people or handle problems, she has been heard to say, "lack of planning on your part doesn't mean an emergency on my part."

Tom

When not engrossed in his own projects, Tom is making the office more efficient and spearheading new—often automated—systems to make things faster and more reliable so each person can get their work done. Tom was trained as an engineer, and his work demonstrates much independent thought. He knows it isn't enough to have a progressive idea or worthy goal; you have to find a way— the time, resources, and skills—to implement it.

Identifying Others

Nina — Two Computer Scientists — Jake

Nina is generally quiet and quite busy—a real problem solver. As a retired army major, high school teacher and part time inventor, she has developed methodologies for many tasks, such as programming. She is very systematic, and teaches her students the same: "create a framework where you can progress from beginning to end." Reading, camping, her family, and two close friends are all else she needs. She feels she does more than she ever dreamed.

Jake is about passionate ideas, promising projects, and interesting people. With computer technology, there is so much to try out, talk out, explore, and develop in any one day that when bursts of motivation—or deadlines—come, he's often hard-pressed to pick just one. Fortunately, even when working alone, he has lots of energy and can handle three jobs at once if called on. Although Jake can be blunt at times, he is known as an inventive promoter and engineer.

Ross — Two Outside Salespersons — Heather

With each of his many clients, Ross gets a clear picture of what's going on, figures out what he has that they need, and then helps them fill that need. He always has a respectful, interested attitude, although sometimes "sales" means helping people get past insecurity and hesitation. He can coordinate the whole picture for clients who have many needs, and can work with other vendors. Ross enjoys life's good things but is also very serious about his goals and works hard.

Heather works at a new international company dealing with environmental products. That's worth it right there. She's really skilled at maintaining smooth connections with customers and hesitates to use any method or procedure that is forced or off-putting. She is pretty good with relationships, often remembering a lot of important details, and people are often amazed by how much she keeps in her head. Really knowing and having expertise with the product is also essential.

Kurt — Two Entertainers — Phineas

Kurt is a musician. He is down to earth and keeps to himself and his friends and has enjoyed playing practically all his life. With his music, Kurt doesn't put into the public sphere anything that he isn't completely comfortable and happy with, that he hasn't actualized to the best it can be. He pulls together each piece as a theme out of his whole life. Kurt's "river" runs deep, and unless his principles are violated, he is a strong friend to those around him.

Phineas often finds himself at the center of what's interesting. He uses acting and music to express the many facets of life that inspire him and the good relationships of all kinds that have moved him. He is comfortable with total strangers, and is often happy helping people he has identified as intelligent and promising. This doesn't mean he's always "on." He enjoys a mellow atmosphere and needs inspiration, and the really creative part of his work demands private thought.

What to Look For

Observing and considering situations from multiple perspectives is a valuable application. Remember that some people will be harder to identify than others.

1. Observe or ask *why* someone is doing something, not just how—what do they want out of the interaction? A person's current energy level, work or social role, or phase of life may alter behavior, but the core desire remains the same.

2. Each interaction style leads, plans, motivates, integrates, and so on in its own ways. For example, a Chart-the-Course style might have learned a method to "act" In-Charge. So consider if there is this kind of learned behavior.

3. Each interaction style likes to "get what it gives." For example, a Get-Things-Going style likes to be inspired as well as proactively inspiring others. People create what they need and are most open to what's natural to them.

4. Clarify work position, learning level, and social roles. A leader or expert position requires that a person "work" their style in a different way than a follower or novice. To find the core style, observe how the person maintains balance under stress.

Perspective Shifting

One of the most powerful ways to apply your understanding of interaction styles is to recognize when your style doesn't match the person you are interacting with, then to shift your perspective to understand the other person and shift your communications to match theirs.

Energy-Shifting Tips

To be effective in our interactions, we often need to shift our energy to match the other person's. Pay attention to how other people are responding to you. Watch their reactions by noticing their voices. Is there tension? Are they relaxed? Are they seemingly open or closed in their posture? Look at the expression on their faces.

Each Interaction Style has a tendency to emphasize some stages and neglect others. Be sure not to neglect any of the stages.

Chart-the-Course	Behind-the-Scenes
• May jump to explaining, getting feedback, answering questions, and leave taking. • May neglect the greeting stage and the getting information stage.	• May focus most on getting information, explaining, and answering questions. • May neglect the more direct ways of getting someone to do something and the leave taking.

In-Charge	Get-Things-Going
• May jump to explaining something, doing something, and getting someone to do something. • May neglect the greeting stage, especially in ongoing relationships in time-pressured situations.	• May overdo the greeting with too much enthusiasm and spend too much time on getting information, getting feedback, and answering questions. • May prolong the interaction and neglect the leave taking.

Aspects of an Interaction

Interaction with others is not as linear as it seems. Every interaction includes ongoing feedback to each participant. Thus each communication is both a stimulus for a new message and a response to the previous message. Yet it is useful to artificially dissect an interaction and identify some kinds of exchanges that can go on.

- **Greeting**—In the very first interaction with someone, the greeting sets the tone for defining the entire relationship. It is the first impression, yet it is never based on a completely blank slate. We bring role expectations based on the context and our past, as well as our natural interaction style tendencies. Even ongoing relationships need a greeting stage to take the measure of where someone is before going on.

- **Getting Information**—Many interactions revolve around information gathering. Each style brings natural resistances to giving information, and it helps to match people at their energy level. Likewise, each style makes certain contributions to getting information. Use the matrix to help you shift your style according to the needs of the person and the situation.

- **Explaining Something**—People expect things to be explained in their style. Our style of explaining may very well determine whether someone listens and understands. Use the matrix to get people to listen and understand.

- **Doing Something**—Interactions often involve doing something to someone or with someone. Style really makes a difference in how comfortable and responsive people are with each other.

- **Getting Feedback or Answering Questions**—Getting feedback goes beyond getting information and requires a higher trust level that the person will take and/or use the feedback well. How you answer questions will help build this trust.

- **Getting Someone to Do Something**—This is the test of one's influencing ability. While the words you say may vary according to someone's interests and other personality factors, the style in which you say them can either evoke resistance and non-compliance or compliance and enthusiastic buy-in.

- **Leave Taking**—How you take leave of someone builds rapport for the next interaction. People of different styles have different preferences at this stage. The last impression is often as important as the first impression.

> **REMEMBER**
>
> In Western culture, there is an expectation that males will exhibit more directing behavior and females will exhibit more informing behavior. Keeping this in mind may help you have more influence as you shift to the culturally expected styles or go counter to them when needed. For example, a Behind-the-Scenes female may need to seem much more In-Charge than a male of the same style in order to counter the cultural bias.

Perspective Shifting

Communication Stages Map™

| | **In-Charge**
Time and Task
Faster Pace
This style prefers... | **Chart-the-Course**
Time and Task
Slower Pace
This style prefers... | **Get-Things-Going**
Enrolling and Relating
Faster Pace
This style prefers... | **Behind-the-Scenes**
Enrolling and Relating
Slower Pace
This style prefers... |
|---|---|---|---|---|
| **Greeting** | • Use a brief cordial opening
• Make direct eye contact
• Use a fast pace
• Speak in a strong voice
• Show confidence
• State directly why you are there | • Use a brief opening
• Make intermittent eye contact
• Have a casual, yet erect posture
• Keep your distance and don't invade their space
• State why you are there | • Use a warm voice tone
• Be expressive
• Make personal comments
• Use open gestures
• Make eye contact
• Be energetic, even jovial in manner | • Use a quietly friendly tone
• Disclose something about yourself
• Try low-key connecting with some eye contact
• Use a slow, calm pace |
| **Getting Information** | • Ask directly
• Be matter of fact
• Don't be too personal
• They may want to know why you need the information | • Limit small talk
• Be matter of fact and less personal
• Pause
• Don't interrupt
• Step back a little | • Be prepared to listen
• Be very responsive, verbally and non-verbally
• Ask open-ended questions
• Speak with an upward inflection | • Don't rush them
• Don't interrupt
• Take pauses
• Use head nods and "un-huh's"
• Speak with an upward inflection |
| **Explaining Something** | • Explain the goal
• Give the reason for the procedure, the timing, etc.
• Present main points, not details unless asked | • Be systematic
• Explain the plan in detail
• Invite questions about the details
• Pause for questions | • Present the main points
• Allow time for conversation and questions
• Be supportive | • Allow reflection time
• Gage them non-verbally and then invite questions or their thoughts |
| **Doing Something** | • Be businesslike
• Be efficient
• If you must redo something, explain why
• Answer questions | • Stay focused on the task at hand
• Answer questions, but don't feel compelled to make small talk
• Be thorough | • Carry on small talk while working to convey interest and caring | • Have a helpful attitude
• Be alert to their need to process and get more information |
| **Getting Feedback or Answering Questions** | • Ask for exactly what you want
• Don't digress, yet stay friendly
• Answer confidently and directly
• If you don't have the answers, assure them you'll get them ASAP
• They are not likely to accept roadblocks to what they see is needed | • Don't rush them
• Reflect back to them what you hear
• Pause
• Don't interrupt
• If you don't have specific answers, don't try to answer generally
• Use active listening
• Say "Oh? (pause) So? (pause)" | • Acknowledge and encourage them to express emotion
• Allow them to digress and ramble as they think out loud
• Say "Oh? (pause) So? (pause)"
• Be verbally and non-verbally responsive and expressive | • Take it slow
• Don't finish their sentences
• Reflect back to them what you heard
• Say "Oh? (pause) So? (pause)"
• Answer questions honestly and openly |
| **Getting Someone to Do Something** | • Tell in a straightforward manner
• Give time-and-task details
• Focus on expected results | • Don't rush them
• Tell in a straightforward manner
• Give an opportunity for them to question
• Pause | • Explore options
• Add elements of fun
• Use storytelling and examples of others | • Get their input
• Be supportive
• Assure them they are not bothering you |
| **Leave Taking** | • Convey a sense of composure and that things are under control
• Pleasantly honor their sense of urgency | • Convey a sense that things are on track and under control
• Be brief, yet assuring | • Show warmth
• Gently close the conversation | • Use caring and gentle friendliness
• Gently close the conversation |

Understanding Yourself and Others®: An Introduction to Interaction Styles

Perspective Shifting

Interaction Styles and Stress

Interaction Style-related stress is not the same as the everyday stress of overwork, overindulgence, and worries over money, relationships, and so on. It results from the core drives of the interaction style patterns not being fulfilled. As with most stress, it is worse when we are unaware of its sources. Knowledge of one's own interaction style can help manage and even prevent such stress.

Chart-the-Course	Behind-the-Scenes
CORE DRIVE To have a plan of action To see movement and progress	**CORE DRIVE** To get the needed or wanted result To integrate and harmonize
STRESSORS Not knowing what is likely to happen Don't see progress	**STRESSORS** Not enough input or credit Pressed to decide too quickly
WHEN STRESSED Withdraw Shut down Insistent involvement	**WHEN STRESSED** Become quiet and agreeable Avoid conflict Take a rigid stance
HOW TO HELP Be calm and direct Let them know what to expect, and update on progress being made Be patient as they express thoughts	**HOW TO HELP** Be friendly, but not too expressive Patiently provide information and encouragement Give time to reflect and integrate
In-Charge	**Get-Things-Going**
CORE DRIVE To get results To see action taken	**CORE DRIVE** To involve and be involved To move things along
STRESSORS Feel out of control Nothing being accomplished	**STRESSORS** Not being a part of what's going on Feel unliked or not accepted
WHEN STRESSED Are bossy and demanding Have outbursts of anger or blame Resentfully check out	**WHEN STRESSED** Feel scattered and panicky Are overly expressive Use selective avoidance
HOW TO HELP Tell them the reasons for things Help them see that something is being done and by when Join them in their humor	**HOW TO HELP** Listen as they talk things out Encourage their active participation Express your own ideas, thoughts, feelings

Interaction Style-related stress is often triggered by a mismatch between the requirements of the situation and one's natural energy pattern. It can also be triggered by conflicting styles in an ongoing relationship. There are some typical responses to this kind of stress, some more effective than others. Yet these responses usually increase the stress.

Sliding over or down to the style that is adjacent on the matrix can be a sign of mild stress as one tries to be more flexible in responding, yet the unconscious stress can make it a slide into negative aspects of the slid-into style. For example, a Get-Things-Going co-worker drops hints to be included in meetings. This negative side of a Behind-the-Scenes style backfires because others perceive it as manipulative.

We often attempt to increase the use of our natural style, with more insistence on its being the right solution. What was once a strength in influencing becomes a liability in the relationship. For example, an In-Charge partner in a business was frustrated by his partner's indecision and kept pushing for action right away, which led the partner to become more stubborn in delaying the decision. Or a Chart-the-Course individual increases her natural disengaging to devise a plan and when she can't get alignment with the plan, completely withdraws from the group.

Flipping over (or out!) to the totally opposite style often happens after an attempt to solve the problem from the natural style is unsuccessful For example a Behind-the-Scenes executive keeps trying to integrate more input from more sources before making important decisions. As the time frame shortens, she flips into a very rigid stance in a bossy, In-Charge manner, resulting in a lower quality decision.

Handling Stress

Stress often results from interpersonal conflict. If the people you are interacting with show a stress response of a particular style, use the chart at left to shift your behavior to match their needs. Reducing their stress may help you use your diversity rather than fight it.

If your own stress results from a mismatch between the demands of the situation, plan your interactions to manage the most draining activities and not let them deplete your energy and negatively affect your performance. Use the matrix to guide you.

Trying to match or flex to the style that is opposite diagonally on the matrix takes the most energy. If a situation requires the diagonally opposite behavior, carefully plan for it or even rehearse it. If you will need to sustain that energy for a long time, be sure to get plenty of rest.

Where Do You Go From Here?

Honor the Differences in Yourself

Just recognizing that people have different energy patterns and approaches to influencing others can make a tremendous difference in your life.

- Avoid the BLT syndrome (Be Like Them). Recognize that you have your own style of leading and influencing. Nurture it and own it.
- Become aware of what situations energize you and which ones drain you.
- Take action to change your life situation so you are in those energizing situations more than the draining ones.

Honor the Differences in Others

Keep in mind that the ways others respond are not bad. They are just not the ways you respond.

- Avoid BLM Syndrome (Be Like Me)—Don't expect everyone to be like you.
- Acknowledge the different drives, core beliefs, and aims of their style.
- Adapt to the style of others. It will not be manipulative if you remember to honor their points of view. It will help you communicate toward a more mutually rewarding relationship.

Welcome the Diversity

Seek all perspectives. Diversity makes any project or group effort more successful. All roles are necessary.

- Someone needs to be In-Charge, out in front taking the lead and making sure results are accomplished.
- Someone needs to Chart-the-Course, outside the picture, making a plan of action and monitoring progress along the way.
- Someone needs to Get-Things-Going, in the middle of it all, inspiring people to action and involving others in the process.
- Someone needs to be Behind-the-Scenes integrating input, finding value in contributions and controlling for the best result possible.

If the role you are playing doesn't match the requirements of the situation, shift your energy to play a different role. If it doesn't match your style, recognize it may take more energy to shift. However, when shifting is consciously done, it is less stressful than if you feel at the mercy of the situation.

If you are in conflict with someone, it may be due to a style difference. Shift your perspective and match his or her style to move to a different level of interaction.

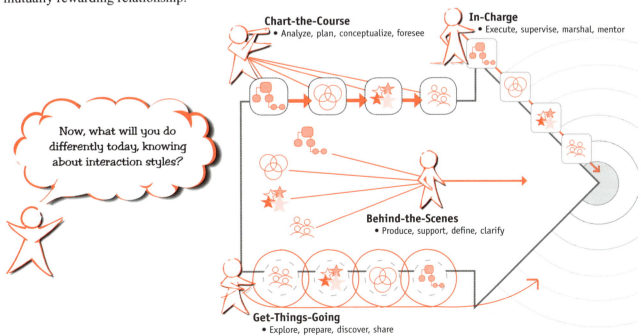

Now, what will you do differently today, knowing about interaction styles?

Chart-the-Course
- Analyze, plan, conceptualize, foresee

In-Charge
- Execute, supervise, marshal, mentor

Behind-the-Scenes
- Produce, support, define, clarify

Get-Things-Going
- Explore, prepare, discover, share

Understanding Yourself and Others®: An Introduction to Interaction Styles

Appendix A: Essential Qualities of Personality Patterns

Essential Qualities of the Personality Patterns
by Linda V. Berens

The 16 Personality Types
(For a complete explanation of the sixteen personality types, see the References for *The 16 Personality Types: Descriptions for Self-Discovery*.)

Sixteen personality patterns have been observed over time from various perspectives and theoretical bases. Each of these patterns has a theme of its own.

The 16 Personality Type Patterns			
Foreseer Developer	Harmonizer Clarifier	Planner Inspector	Protector Supporter
Envisioner Mentor	Discoverer Advocate	Implementor Supervisor	Facilitator Caretaker
Conceptualizer Director	Designer Theorizer	Analyzer Operator	Composer Producer
Strategist Mobilizer	Explorer Inventor	Promoter Executor	Motivator Presenter

We use three lenses to look at the sixteen types—Temperament, Interaction Styles, and Cognitive Dynamics. Each lens provides different information about personality. Sometimes it is useful to explore each lens on its own. Other times two lenses are used together for a more complete picture. The three lenses taken together give the fullest picture and provide the most information.

Temperament
(For a complete explanation of Temperament Theory, see the References for *Understanding Yourself and Others®: An Introduction to Temperament*.)

Temperament Theory is based in descriptions of behavior that go back over twenty-five centuries. It tells us the "why" of behavior, our motivators, and sources of deep psychological stress. Knowing our temperament patterns tells us our core needs and values as well as the talents we are more likely to be drawn to develop. Temperament gives us four broad themes in a pattern of core psychological needs, core values, talents, and behaviors—all of which are interrelated.

The four temperament patterns also have qualities in common with each other and can be described in those terms as well.

Abstract versus Concrete language—the way we tend to think about things and the way we use words. The Idealist and Rational patterns are characterized by abstract language with a focus on intangibles—concepts, ideas, implications, and meaning. People with these patterns as primary seek to know or explain the meaning of something that is not seen in order to access information that is not obvious. The Guardian and Artisan temperament patterns are characterized by concrete language with a focus on tangibles—experiences and observations. Those with these patterns seek to get or give useful concrete information to plan for the future of take action in the present.

Affiliative versus Pragmatic roles—the way we prefer to interact with others. The Idealist and Guardian patterns are more Affiliative in nature, with a focus on interdependence, human and group effectiveness, inclusion, agreement, and sanction. The Rational and Artisan patterns are more Pragmatic in nature with a focus on independence and operational effectiveness, self-determination, autonomous actions, and expedience.

The Four Temperament Patterns			
	ABSTRACT		**CONCRETE**
AFFILIATIVE	**IDEALIST** ABSTRACT/AFFILIATIVE Meaning and Significance Unique Identity DIPLOMATIC—Clarifying, Unifying, Individualizing, and Inspiring		**GUARDIAN** CONCRETE/AFFILIATIVE Membership or Belonging Responsibility or Duty LOGISTICAL—Organizing, Facilitating, Checking, and Supporting
PRAGMATIC	**RATIONAL** ABSTRACT/PRAGMATIC Mastery and Self-Control Knowledge and Competence STRATEGIC—Engineering, Conceptualizing, Theorizing, and Coordinating		**ARTISAN** CONCRETE/PRAGMATIC Freedom to Act Ability to Make an Impact TACTICAL—Actions, Composing, Producing, and Motivating

Appendix A: Essential Qualities of Personality Patterns

Another dimension not shown on the matrix is the focus on Structure versus Motive—where we focus our attention when interacting with others. The Rational and Guardian patterns are characterized by a focus on structure, order, and organization to gain a measure of control over life's problems and irregularities rather than be at the mercy of random forces. The Idealist and Artisan patterns are characterized by a focus on motives and why people do things in order to work with the people they are communicating with rather than trying to force them into a preconceived structure.

Of the three lenses, temperament is the broadest and each temperament pattern describes the driving force of four of the sixteen types.

Interaction Styles

Interaction Styles is based on observable behavior patterns that are quite similar to the popular social styles models and DISC®. Interaction Styles tells us the "how" of our behavior. It refers to patterns of interaction that are both highly contextual and yet innate. Knowing our interaction style helps us locate interpersonal conflicts and situational energy drains. It gives us a map for greater flexibility in our interactions with others.

These four interaction style patterns are characterized by different interactional dynamics. Those dynamics are Directing/Informing and Initiating/Responding.

The *Directing* style has a time and task focus with a tendency to direct the actions of others to accomplish a task in accordance with deadlines, often by either telling or asking. Regarding motivations and process, the Directing style is explicit.

The opposite style is *Informing*, with a motivation and process focus. Using this style, people tend to give information in order to enroll others in the process. When a task needs to be accomplished, the Informing style engages others, describing outcomes and processes that can be used to complete the task.

Each style has its own best and appropriate use, and most people use both at different times but have more comfort with one.

Each of these patterns can also be further differentiated by another dimension—a preference for either *Initiating* interactions and a faster pace or for *Responding* to interactions and a slower pace. The four different interaction style patterns are shown in the matrix to the above right.

The Four Interaction Style Patterns

	DIRECTING	INFORMING
RESPONDING	**CHART-THE-COURSE** DIRECTING/RESPONDING Push for a plan of action Keep the group on track Deliberate decisions Define the process focus	**BEHIND-THE-SCENES** INFORMING/RESPONDING Push for the best result Support the group's process Consultative decisions Understand the process focus
INITIATING	**IN-CHARGE** DIRECTING/INITIATING Push for completion Lead the group to the goal Quick decisions Results focus	**GET-THINGS-GOING** INFORMING/INITIATING Push for involvement Facilitate the group's process Enthusiastic decisions Interaction focus

Cognitive Dynamics

(For a complete explanation of Cognitive Dynamics, see the reference for *Dynamics of Personality Type: Understanding and Applying Jung's Cognitive Processes*.)

Cognitive Dynamics is based in the Jungian theory from which the Myers-Briggs Type Indicator® (MBTI®) is derived. Each of the sixteen types has a theme based in a unique dynamic pattern of cognitive processes and their development. Knowing our innate tendencies to use these processes in certain ways can help us release blocks to our creativity and to effective communication. This model provides us the key to growth and development.

Carl Jung's Theory of Psychological Type

In examining individual differences, Swiss psychiatrist Carl Jung differentiated two fundamentally different orientations. He noticed some people seem primarily oriented to the world outside themselves. He called these people *extraverted*. He saw other people as primarily oriented to the world inside themselves. He called these people *introverted*. This extraverted-introverted difference is related to where you focus and recharge your energy. Then Jung noticed that people could be further distinguished by their preferred mental processes. Jung saw two kinds of mental processes used in everyday life: the process of *perception* (becoming aware of) and the process of *judgment* (organizing or deciding).

He then further differentiated two kinds of perception—*Sensation* and *Intuition*. *Sensing* is a process of becoming aware of sensory information. *Intuiting** is a

---

* We use *Sensing* and *Intuiting* to refer to mental processes rather than *Sensation* and *Intuition*, which refer to names of something. Our focus is on the activity, not the "type."

Appendix A: Essential Qualities of Personality Patterns

process of becoming aware of abstract pattern information and meanings. Both kinds of information are available to us, but we pay attention to only one kind at a time. Both are necessary and valuable in everyday life.

Likewise, he noted two kinds of judgment—*Thinking* and *Feeling*. Thinking judgments are based on objective criteria and are detached from personal values. Feeling judgments are based on subjective considerations and are attached to personal and universal values. Even the smallest act involves either Thinking or Feeling judgments, and both kinds of decisions are needed and valuable.

Each of these four mental processes can be used in either the external world of extraversion or the internal world of introversion, producing eight mental processes. Then Jung outlined eight psychological types, each characterized by the predominance of one of these eight mental processes (extraverted Sensing, introverted Sensing, extraverted iNtuiting, introverted iNtuiting, extraverted Thinking, introverted Thinking, extraverted Feeling, and introverted Feeling). In his writings he suggested that each of these eight dominant mental processes was supported by one of two opposing processes and that each of these eight types might vary according to which opposite mental process was used in support of the dominant. For example, the extraverted Sensing type with Thinking would be somewhat different from the extraverted Sensing type with Feeling. Thus, his notions imply sixteen type patterns, each characterized by preferences for the use of two of the eight mental *processes,* as shown in the table to the left.

Enter Measurement and the Four-Letter Code

When Isabel Myers began developing the MBTI, she faced several challenges. One challenge was the beginning of the self-report movement. Prior to that time, psychologists doubted that a self-report format would work. Also, it was a time of "measurement," and the scientific thinking of the time was to understand the world by dividing it into parts. Myers faced the challenge of keeping the holistic quality of Jung's types in the forefront, while meeting the demands of the tests and measurement world. She chose to focus on the opposites in Jung's theory. Jung said that the orientations of extraversion and introversion were dynamically opposite. You can't be in two places at one time! He also said the mental processes were dynamically opposite. Thus, one would have a preference for either Sensing or iNtuiting and Thinking or Feeling in one's day-to-day interactions. The genius of Isabel Myers (and her mother, Katharine Briggs) was to develop questions about everyday actions and choices that reflected these underlying opposing preferences.

When the preferences for each of these pairs of opposites were indicated, then the type pattern could be inferred. However, a difficulty remained in how to determine which mental process was dominant in the personality and which was auxiliary. Myers reasoned that we can more readily observe what we do externally, so she decided to add questions to try to find which preferred mental process individuals used in the external world. If they used their preferred judging process to order the external world, they would be likely to make lists and structure their time in advance. If they used their preferred perceiving process to experience the external world, they would avoid such planning and structuring and prefer to keep things open-ended. Thus, the Judging-Perceiving scale of the MBTI was born. The resultant four-letter code is used around the world to give people insights about themselves.

Type Dynamics and Development

Type dynamics is based on the theories of Carl Jung and refers to a hierarchy of cognitive processes (Sensing, iNtuiting, Thinking, Feeling) and a preference for being either in the external world (extraversion) or the internal world (introversion). Type dynamics and type development refer to the unfolding of the personality pattern as expressed through the development of the

The Four Sensing Types

extraverted **Sensing**	with introverted Thinking	(ESTP)
extraverted **Sensing**	with introverted Feeling	(ESFP)
introverted **Sensing**	with extraverted Thinking	(ISTJ)
introverted **Sensing**	with extraverted Feeling	(ISFJ)

The Four iNtuiting Types

extraverted **iNtuiting**	with introverted Thinking	(ENTP)
extraverted **iNtuiting**	with introverted Feeling	(ENFP)
introverted **iNtuiting**	with extraverted Thinking	(INTJ)
introverted **iNtuiting**	with extraverted Feeling	(INFJ)

The Four Thinking Types

introverted **Thinking**	with extraverted Sensing	(ISTP)
introverted **Thinking**	with extraverted iNtuiting	(INTP)
extraverted **Thinking**	with introverted Sensing	(ESTJ)
extraverted **Thinking**	with introverted iNtuiting	(ENTJ)

The Four Feeling Types

introverted **Feeling**	with extraverted Sensing	(ISFP)
introverted **Feeling**	with extraverted iNtuiting	(INFP)
extraverted **Feeling**	with introverted Sensing	(ESFJ)
extraverted **Feeling**	with introverted iNtuiting	(ENFJ)

Appendix A: Essential Qualities of Personality Patterns

mental processes of perception and judgment. Since the personality is a living system, it is self-organizing—self-maintaining, self-transcending, and self-renewing. Growth and development follow principles of organic development, and there is an order to the evolution of the personality.

The first cognitive process to develop and become more refined is often called the dominant. It is the favorite. The second is often called the auxiliary because it "helps" the first one. It develops second (usually between the ages of twelve to twenty). Development of the third process usually begins around age twenty and continues until age thirty-five or so. The fourth or least preferred process usually comes into play more between the ages of thirty-five to fifty. These developmental ages are general, not fixed. At these times, we find ourselves drawn to activities that engage and utilize the processes.

Thus we can say that development is dynamic and growing. Development in this sense is like readiness to learn to talk or to walk. We don't have to make children do these, we only need to provide models and opportunities and then stay out of the way. Development can be diverted due to environmental pressures and so is not always in this order as we develop some "proficiencies" using these cognitive processes. Still, the innate preference pattern will remain the same.

Using the MBTI®

In looking at how the models relate to the MBTI, it is important to remember that the results of any instrument are just an artificial snapshot in time. Also, an instrument is not the theory. The results of an instrument are neither the whole of a theory nor the whole of a personality. This is why ethical and competent users of the MBTI follow the person-to-person feedback standards of self-selection and validation by the client. One must not assume the results of the MBTI (or any other instrument) are 100 percent accurate. They must always be validated through an exploratory process such as we describe in this book.

How Do the Models Relate?

The temperament patterns (extended out to the four variations of each) meet Jung's theory at the level of the sixteen type patterns. The four-letter codes produced by the MBTI, when they are accurate and verified for individuals, match Keirsey's sixteen type patterns. While at first glance the matching process looks illogical, it occurs at a deep theoretical level when comparing Jung's and Kretschmer's original works. More importantly, it occurs on a descriptive, behavioral level. Following, is The Temperament Matrix with the sixteen themes, Interaction Styles, the four-letter MBTI codes, and the type dynamics patterns represented by the type code. (The dominant is listed first, auxiliary second, tertiary third, and inferior fourth.)

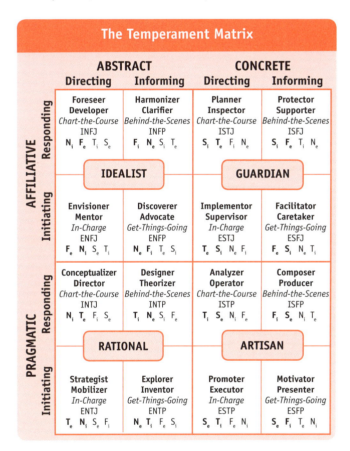

Answers for Identifying Others from pages 26–27:

Marilyn—Get-Things-Going
Linda—Behind-the-Scenes
Diana—In-Charge
Nina—Chart-the-Course
Ross—In-Charge
Kurt—Behind-the-Scenes
Madeline—Chart-the-Course
Mike—In-Charge
Tom—Chart-the-Course
Jake—Get-Things-Going
Heather—Behind-the-Scenes
Phineas—Get-Things-Going

Appendix B: Frequently Asked Questions

Frequently Asked Questions

Why don't the Interaction Styles match the Myers-Briggs letters in some parallel fashion?

The relationships between the two models were revealed by a matching of patterns derived from the different models independently. Each lens or model allows looking at the whole in different ways yet ignores the differences that might relate to other models. You can see the underlying logic when you remember that the MBTI code does not stand for a collection of traits that go with the four separate indices. Jung's original work was based on eight holistic types, each characterized by a difference mental process (see Appendix A). Fundamental to a holistic view is the understanding that trying to understand an organic whole by looking at the "parts" is an artificial distinction and the whole can never be fully understood through the parts.

Why do you say these styles are inborn?

Almost all of the related models suggest that these styles or types are inborn in some way, even if they focus on outer behavior. Ongoing studies have been conducted on the various "temperamental" traits that can be identified and tracked over time with physiological measures. Most notable of these are the extensive longitudinal studies of temperament traits by Stella Chess and Alexander Thomas. Their research extends over 50 years and tracks some of their subjects from as young as three months well into adulthood.

Robert Ornstein summarized research on these traits as three dimensions of temperament in *Roots of the Self*. In Ornstein's view, temperament refers to the style of our behavior, not the content of our behavior. (This definition is different than David Keirsey's definition of temperament.) Ornstein laid to rest the nature-nurture question by clearly stating that our behavior is determined by our nature, our past experiences, and the current context. Ornstein identified three main dimensions of temperament that have been measured physiologically and observed clinically:

1. **Cortical arousal**
   How much external stimulation it takes to arouse the brain is seen as an indicator of how much internal activity is already going on. Some seem to need very little external stimulation and like to have a slower pace of input and more reflection time. Others seem to need a lot of activity and stimulation. He relates this directly to introversion and extraversion respectively.

2. **Regulation and organization of actions as in deliberation versus liberation**
   Some people seem to need to structure and organize their actions and their thoughts. Others seem to need a maximum amount of freedom from boundaries. This dimension also relates to how freely emotions will be expressed or controlled. This continuum ranges from extreme planners who plan every detail, to extreme free spirits who abhor plans.

3. **Feeling tone as in approach versus withdrawal**
   This dimension seems to have to do with which emotions are part of our make-up. Positive ones make us want to approach others and negative ones make us want to withdraw. The continuum here seems to go from extreme hyperactive elation to extreme immobilizing sadness.

These three dimensions are remarkably similar to the dimensions outlined by William Marston in the 1920s and the Social Style proponents.

How do you know these models are interrelated and the descriptions accurate?

I noticed that descriptions in the DiSC® and the Social Styles models had many similarities to the interaction style patterns we had been observing in relation to the sixteen types identified by the Myers-Briggs four letter code. Conceptual research led me to consult many original sources of descriptions. Most of these sources seemed to be describing patterns that also included aspects of Keirsey's temperament patterns. When I filtered out temperament descriptors and looked at what seemed to be just the interaction patterns, I found characteristics that fit all four types (different temperaments) that shared each Interaction Style pattern.

From this research on other models and years of observations of the sixteen types as thematic wholes, themes were identified and descriptions drafted to describe each of the four interaction styles. To draft the self-portraits, we used the transcripts from the interviews used to develop the sixteen type descriptions in which four people of each type responded to the question, "What is it like to be you?" This provided the language of each style. The descriptions were validated by feedback from several people of each type who read the descriptions.

Links to Other Models

Keirseyan Temperament Theory

About 1985, David Keirsey identified role directing and role informing differences in his four temperament patterns. Thus he named two variants of each temperament. Later, he clarified, in a lecture, that there was another interactional dynamic that he called Initiating and Responding and later referred to as public and private. This latter dynamic clearly related to Extraversion and Introversion, not only as defined by Jung, but also as defined by the physiological psychologists.

Temperament theory derives from organismic psychology, which considers organic wholes rather than looking at separate traits. It also is strongly based in the work of Gregory Bateson on communication theory and family systems theory. This latter work, taken further by Paul Watzlawick, focuses on the relationship-defining aspects of communication, which is why Keirsey called the differences role directing and role informing.

Myers-Briggs Type Indicator®

Various aspects of Jungian-based typology relate either directly or indirectly to the Interaction Style patterns and dynamics. The matches to the full type patterns are listed on the matrix to the right.

The connections between Initiating and Extraversion and between Responding and Introversion are conceptually very clear. In fact when the MBTI Step II was developed through factor analysis, a very similar subscale emerged. However, the Initiating and Responding dynamics are not the whole of Jung's notion of Extraversion/Introversion.

Directing communications seem to have a task focus and Informing communications have a people focus. MBTI practitioners have long related task focus to a preference for Thinking and people focus to a preference for Feeling. Likewise, one would assume that a time focus goes with a preference for Judging and an emergence focus goes with a preference for Perceiving. Yet, when Keirsey applied the role-directing versus role informing construct to the sixteen types as they related to temperament, he related Directing to N and J or S and T in the type code and Informing to N and P or S and F in the type code. Our investigations bore out Keirsey's distinctions.

Interaction Styles and Temperament and the MBTI®

	DIRECTING		INFORMING	
RESPONDING	TEMPERAMENT IDEALIST / MBTI® TYPE CODE INFJ	TEMPERAMENT GUARDIAN / MBTI® TYPE CODE ISTJ	TEMPERAMENT IDEALIST / MBTI® TYPE CODE INFP	TEMPERAMENT GUARDIAN / MBTI® TYPE CODE ISFJ
	CHART-THE-COURSE		**BEHIND-THE-SCENES**	
	TEMPERAMENT RATIONAL / MBTI® TYPE CODE INTJ	TEMPERAMENT ARTISAN / MBTI® TYPE CODE ISTP	TEMPERAMENT RATIONAL / MBTI® TYPE CODE INTP	TEMPERAMENT ARTISAN / MBTI® TYPE CODE ISFP
INITIATING	TEMPERAMENT IDEALIST / MBTI® TYPE CODE ENFJ	TEMPERAMENT GUARDIAN / MBTI® TYPE CODE ESTJ	TEMPERAMENT IDEALIST / MBTI® TYPE CODE ENFP	TEMPERAMENT GUARDIAN / MBTI® TYPE CODE ESFJ
	IN-CHARGE		**GET-THINGS-GOING**	
	TEMPERAMENT RATIONAL / MBTI® TYPE CODE ENTJ	TEMPERAMENT ARTISAN / MBTI® TYPE CODE ESTP	TEMPERAMENT RATIONAL / MBTI® TYPE CODE ENTP	TEMPERAMENT ARTISAN / MBTI® TYPE CODE ESFP

DiSC®

In 1928, William Marston wrote about the emotional basis for our behavior. Emotions are both psychological and physiological events. Marston focused on what he saw as "the motor self" or a sort of motor or muscular predisposition to react to different environmental stimuli in certain ways. For Marston an emotion involves an urge to move in some fashion. He distinguished emotion from feelings which he considered perceptions. He identified four primary emotions, each with an initial feeling tone of either pleasantness or unpleasantness:

- Dominance, with a feeling of unpleasantness until stimulus is acted upon
- Compliance, with a feeling of unpleasantness until stimulus is reconciled
- Inducement, with a feeling of pleasantness increasing as interaction increases
- Submission, with a feeling of pleasantness increasing as yielding increases

John Geier picked up Marston's work and out of it developed the DiSC® instrument. Geier's interest was one of looking at traits and clusters of traits that would

Appendix C: Links to Other Models

help us understand how we behave in the "social field." In 1997, Geier interpreted Marston's work through a trait cluster lens, looking for source traits. Source traits (from Raymond Cattell's distinctions) can be factor analyzed and seem to have some sort of underlying unity. This unity seems quite similar to the pattern descriptions that come from a holistic view of the organism which is the underlying foundation of the Interaction Style model.

Social Styles

In contrast to Jung, the primary focus of the authors who wrote about social styles was on an individual's outer behavior, not an individual's inner state. Bolton and Bolton give the most comprehensive references to the sources of the social styles model. Many of these trace back in some way to Blake and Mouton's Managerial Grid which describes behavior along a dichotomy of concern for production versus concern for people. Bolton and Bolton give credit to David Merrill and his associates for developing the Social Styles Model. This model is built on two dimensions. One dimension is along a continuum of more assertive to less assertive. The Boltons define assertiveness as forcefulness in interactions. Their descriptions, including taking the initiative in interpersonal relationships and faster versus slower pace, closely relate to Initiating versus Responding. The other dimension of Social Styles is responsiveness to less responsive. They describe those who are more responsive as emotionally responsive or expressive and those who are less responsive as emotionally controlled. The descriptors of this dimension include people versus task focus as well as many postural and movement characteristics. Descriptors of "responsive" seem to go with the Informing style of communication and descriptors of "less responsive" seem to go with the Directing style of communication. The Social Style patterns of Driver, Analytical, Amiable, and Expressive match well the Interaction style patterns. The Boltons even go so far as to break the styles down even further into four subtypes which would closely match the sixteen type patterns. Tony Alessandra described four styles, Director, Thinker, Relater, and Socializer, with dimensions of Open versus Guarded and Direct versus Indirect. He also described sixteen styles.

Thomas-Kilmann Conflict Modes

Kenneth Thomas and Ralph Kilmann developed an instrument and a model for looking at interpersonal conflict. They posited personal predispositions for handling conflict as well as noting that certain conditions require different approaches. They point out that on their instrument, people may respond according to their predispositions or according to ways they've learned to handle conflict situations. The dimensions identified by Thomas and Kilmann—Assertive to Unassertive and Cooperative to Uncooperative—are very similar to the social styles dimensions. Four of their conflict styles—Competing, Avoiding, Accommodating, Collaborating—map well to the four Interaction Styles.

The table lists the DiSC styles, Bolton and Bolton's styles, Alessandra's, and the Thomas-Kilmann Conflict Styles (TKI) along with the corresponding MBTI® Type code. The relationships are based on a match of content and fit of descriptions from the explanations given by the authors, not on instrument results. None of these relationships are perfect matches, yet the essence of each is represented in the interaction styles.

Other Links to Interaction Styles

	DIRECTING		INFORMING	
RESPONDING	Analytical **ANALYTICAL** *Thinking Thinker* INTJ	Amiable **ANALYTICAL** *Relating Thinker* ISTJ	Analytical **AMIABLE** *Thinking Relater* INTP	Amiable **AMIABLE** *Relating Relater* ISFJ
	Chart-the-Course DiSC®: "C" Bolton and Bolton: Analytical Allessandra: Thinker TKI®: Avoiding		**Behind-the-Scenes** DiSC®: "S" Bolton and Bolton: Amiable Allessandra: Relater TKI®: Accommodating	
	Driver **ANALYTICAL** *Directing Thinker* ISTP	Expressive **ANALYTICAL** *Socializing Thinker* INFJ	Driver **AMIABLE** *Directing Relater* ISFP	Expressive **AMIABLE** *Socializing Relater* INFP
INITIATING	Analytical **DRIVER** *Thinking Director* ENTJ	Amiable **DRIVER** *Relating Director* ESTJ	Analytical **EXPRESSIVE** *Thinking Socializer* ENTP	Amiable **EXPRESSIVE** *Relating Socializer* ESFJ
	In-Charge DiSC®: "D" Bolton and Bolton: Driver Allessandra: Director TKI®: Competing		**Get-Things-Going** DiSC®: "i" Bolton and Bolton: Expressive Allessandra: Socializer TKI®: Collaborating	
	Driver **DRIVER** *Directing Director* ESTP	Expressive **DRIVER** *Socializing Director* ENFJ	Driver **EXPRESSIVE** *Directing Socializer* ESFP	Expressive **EXPRESSIVE** *Socializing Socializer* ENFP

Appendix D: Additional Resources

Interaction Styles
Alessandra, Tony, and Michael J. O'Connor. *The Platinum Rule, Discover the Four Basic Business Personalities—and How They Can Lead You to Success*. New York: Warner Books, 1996.

Bolton, Robert, and Dorothy Grover Bolton. *People Styles at Work: Making Bad Relationships Good and Good Relationships Better*. New York: American Management Association, 1996.

Bolton, Robert, and Dorothy Grover Bolton. *Social Style/Management Style: Developing Productive Work Relationships*. New York: American Management Associations, 1984.

Geier, John G. and Dorothy E. Downey. *Energetics of Personality*. Minneapolis: Aristos Publishing House, 1989.

Geier, John G. and Dorothy E. Downey. *Personality Analysis*. Minneapolis: Aristos Publishing House, 1989.

Hunsaker, Phillip L. and Anthony J. Alessandra. *The Art of Managing People*. New York: Simon and Schuster, 1986.

Marston, William Moulton. *Emotions of Normal People*. Minneapolis: Persona Press, [1928]1979.

Tannen, Deborah. *You Just Don't Understand*. New York: William Morrow and Company, 1990.

Watzlawick, Paul; Janet Helmick Beaven and Don D. Jackson. *Pragmatics of Human Communication: A Study of Interactional Patterns, Pathologies, and Paradoxes*. New York: W.W. Norton and Company, 1967.

Biological Basis of Behavior
Chess, Stella, and Alexander Thomas. *Goodness of Fit: Clinical Applications from Infancy Through Adult Life*. Brunner Mazel, 1999.

Colt, George Howe. "Life Special: Were You Born That Way?" *Life* (April 1998): 38–50.

Hamer, Dean, and Peter Copeland. *Living with Our Genes: Why They Matter More Than You Think*. New York: Bantam Doubleday Dell, 1998.

Ornstein, Robert. *The Roots of the Self: Unraveling the Mystery of Who We Are*. San Francisco: HarperCollins, 1993.

Cultural Influences
Hofstede, Geert. *Culture and Organizations: Software of the Mind*. New York: McGraw-Hill, 1997.

Temperament
Berens, Linda V., *Understanding Yourself and Others: An Introduction to Temperament 2.0*. Huntington Beach, Calif.: Telos Publications, 2000.

Delunas, Eve. *Survival Games Personalities Play*. Carmel, Calif.: SunInk Publications, 1992.

Keirsey, David, and Marilyn Bates. *Please Understand Me*. 3d ed. Del Mar, Calif.: Prometheus Nemesis Books, 1978.

Keirsey, David. *Please Understand Me II*. Del Mar, Calif.: Prometheus Nemesis Books, 1998.

Keirsey, David. *Portraits of Temperament*. Del Mar, Calif.: Prometheus Nemesis Books, 1987.

Kretschmer, Ernst. *Physique and Character*. London: Harcourt Brace, 1925.

Nardi, Dario. *Multiple Intelligences and Personality Type: Tools and Strategies for Developing Human Potential*. Huntington Beach, Calif.: Telos Publications, 2001.

Roback, A. A. *The Psychology of Character*. New York: Arno Press, [1927]1973.

Spränger, E. *Types of Men*. New York: Johnson Reprint Company, [1928]1966.

The Sixteen Personality Types
Baron, Renee. *What Type Am I?* New York: Penguin Putnam, 1998.

Berens, Linda V., and Dario Nardi. *The 16 Personality Types: Descriptions for Self-Discovery*. Huntington Beach, Calif.: Telos Publications, 1999.

Fairhurst, Alice M., and Lisa L. Fairhurst. *Effective Teaching, Effective Learning*. Palo Alto, Calif.: Consulting Psychologists Press, 1995.

Isachsen, Olaf, and Linda V. Berens. *Working Together: A Personality Centered Approach to Management*. 3d edition. San Juan Capistrano, Calif.: Institute for Management Development, 1991.

Nardi, Dario. *Character and Personality Type: Discovering Your Uniqueness for Career and Relationship Success*. Huntington Beach, Calif.: Telos Publications, 1999.

Segal, Marci. *Creativity and Personality Type: Tools for Understanding and Inspiring the Many Voices of Creativity*. Huntington Beach, Calif.: Telos Publications, 2001.

Jung/Myers Model
Berens, Linda V. *Dynamics of Personality Type: Understanding and Applying Jung's Cognitive Processes*. Huntington Beach, Calif.: Telos Publications, 1999.

Jung, Carl G. *Psychological Types*. Princeton, N.J.: Princeton University Press, 1971.

Myers, Isabel Briggs, with Peter B. Myers. *Gifts Differing*. Palo Alto, Calif.: Consulting Psychologists Press, [1980]1995.

Myers, Isabel Briggs, Mary H. McCaulley and Naomi L. Quenk. *MBTI Manual: A Guide to the Development and Use of the Myers-Briggs Type Indicator*. Palo Alto, Calif.: Consulting Psychologists Press, 1998.

Sharp, Daryl. *Personality Type: Jung's Model of Typology*. Toronto, Canada: Inner City Books, 1987.

Quenk, Naomi. *In the Grip*. Palo Alto, Calif.: Consulting Psychologists Press, 1985.

Systems Thinking
Bateson, Gregory. *Mind and Nature: A Necessary Unity*. New York: Bantam Books, 1979.

Bateson, Gregory. *Steps to an Ecology of Mind*. New York: Ballantine Books, 1972.

Capra, Fritjof. *The Web of Life*. New York: Anchor Books, Doubleday, 1996.

Goldstein, Kurt. *The Organism*. New York: Zone Books, 1995.

Oshry, Barry. *Seeing Systems: Unlocking the Mysteries of Organizational Life*. San Francisco: Berrett-Koehler Publishers, 1996.

Wheatley, Margaret J. *Leadership and the New Science*. San Francisco: Berrett-Koehler Publishers, 1992.

Applying Multiple Models
Nardi, D., and L. Berens. "Wizards in the Wilderness and the Search for True Type." *Bulletin of Psychological Type* 21, no. 1 (1998). (This article is available on the Temperament Research Institute Web site—http://www.tri-network.com/articles/)

On the Internet
16types.com, http://www.16types.com
Interaction Styles, http://www.interactionstyles.com
Telos Publications, http://www.telospublications.com
TRI, http://www.tri-network.com

Other titles in the
Understanding Yourself and Others® Series

Understand your psychological core needs, natural talents, abilities, and behaviors to gain better awareness of yourself and others in this concise and thorough exploration of the Keirseyan Interaction style Theory.

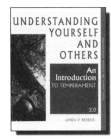

**Understanding Yourself and Others:
An Introduction to Temperament 2.0**
by Linda V. Berens
Retail Price: $5.95
44 Pages
ISBN: 0966462440

**The 16 Personality Types:
Descriptions for Self-Discovery**
by Linda V. Berens and Dario Nardi
Retail Price: $6.95
52 Pages
ISBN: 0966462475

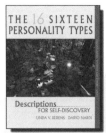

Discover your personality type pattern in this quick and easy read. The authors have captured the essence of the sixteen personality type patterns. An interactive process is provided to help you understand and clarify your "best-fit" personality type.

Paths to personal growth and development are provided to help develop all aspects of your personality pattern. Expand your awareness of personality type diversity through the exploration of sixty-four character biographies and eight life-themes.

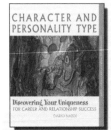

**Character and Personality Type:
Discovering Your Uniqueness for
Career and Relationship Success**
by Dario Nardi
Retail Price: $11.95
76 Pages
ISBN: 0966462467

**Dynamics of Personality Type:
Understanding and Applying
Jung's Cognitive Processes**
by Linda V. Berens
Retail Price: $8.95
60 Pages
ISBN: 0966462459

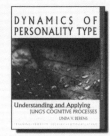

Discover the theory behind the personality type code—Carl Jung's theory of psychological type. Insightful exercises and applications are provided to deepen your understanding and awareness of all eight cognitive processes.

Designed to develop your systems thinking perspective. This book will influence how you view and enter any situation. Intelligence is explored through multiple lenses—personality, Howard Gardner's eight multiple intelligences, and consciousness.

**Multiple Intelligences and Personality Type:
Tools and Strategies
for Developing Human Potential**
by Dario Nardi
Retail Price: $17.95
130 Pages
ISBN: 09664624160

**Creativity and Personality Type:
Tools for Understanding and Inspiring
the Many Voices of Creativity**
by Marci Segal
Retail Price: $19.95
154 Pages
ISBN: 0966462408

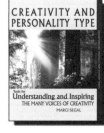

As you inquire into the realm of understanding creativity and discovering your creative voice, you are guided to self-discover your personality type pattern through the models of interaction style and the cognitive processes. Over twenty tools are provided to conduct idea-generating sessions.